ILEX FOUNDATION SERIES 12

COMPARATIVE LITERATURE AND CLASSICAL PERSIAN POETICS

Also in the Ilex Foundation Series

Dreaming across Boundaries:
The Interpretation of Dreams in Islamic Lands
edited by Louise Marlow

Strī: Women in Epic Mahābhārata
by Kevin McGRATH

Persian Literature and Judeo-Persian Culture:
Collected Writings of Sorour S. Soroudi
edited by Houchang Chehabi

The Rhetoric of Biography:
Narrating Lives in Persianate Societies
edited by L. Marlow

Jaya: Performance in Epic Mahābhārata
by Kevin McGRATH

The History *of Beyhaqi (The History of Sultan Masʿud*
of Ghazna, 1030–1041) by Abu'l-Fażl Beyhaqi
translated and with commentaries by Clifford Edmund Bosworth
fully revised and with further commentary by Mohsen Ashtiany

Ruse and Wit:
The Humorous in Arabic, Persian, and Turkish Narrative
edited by Dominic Parviz Brookshaw

The Last of the Rephaim:
Conquest and Cataclysm in the Heroic Ages of Ancient Israel
by Brian R. Doak

Heroic Krsna: Friendship in Epic Mahahabharata
by Kevin McGRATH

On the Wonders of Land and Sea: Persianate Travel Writing
edited by Roberta Micallef and Sunil Sharma

Poet and Hero in the Persian Book of Kings
Third Edition
by Olga M. Davidson

COMPARATIVE LITERATURE AND CLASSICAL PERSIAN POETICS

SECOND EDITION

Olga M. Davidson

Ilex Foundation
Boston, Massachusetts
and
Center for Hellenic Studies
Trustees for Harvard University
Washington, D. C.

Distributed by Harvard University Press
Cambridge, Massachusetts, and London, England

Comparative Literature and Classical Persian Poetics (Second Edition)
By Olga M. Davidson

Published by Ilex Foundation, Boston, Massachusetts and the Center for Hellenic Studies, Trustees for Harvard University, Washington, D.C.

Distributed by Harvard University Press, Cambridge, Massachusetts and London, England

Production editor: Christopher Dadian
Cover design: Joni Godlove
Copyeditor: John McDonald

Printed in the United States of America

On the cover: *Arash-e-kamangar* preparing to release the arrow, which upon landing will mark the border between Iran and Turan. Painting by Mostafa Darehbaghi; private collection of Olga M. Davidson.

Library of Congress Cataloging-in-Publication Data

Davidson, Olga M.
Comparative literature and classical Persian poetics / Olga M. Davidson. -- Second edition.
pages cm. -- (Ilex Foundation series)
Originally published: Costa Mesa, CA: Mazda Publishers, 2000.
Includes bibliographical references and index.
ISBN 978-0-674-07320-3 (alk. paper)
1. Firdawsi. Shahnamah. 2. Comparative literature. 3. Poetics. I. Title.
PK6459.D377 2013
891'.5511--dc23

2013008310

I dedicate this book to my daughter, Antonia

چو غنچه گرچه فروبستگیست کار جهان
تو همچو باد بهاری گره‌گشا میباش

CONTENTS

Preface to the Second Edition

This new edition of Comparative Literature and Classical Persian Poetics supersedes the first edition, published in 2000 by Mazda Press (Costa Mesa CA) as volume 4 of the Intellectual Traditions Series of Bibliotheca Iranica, edited by the late Hossein Ziai. I take this opportunity to record my gratitude to Professor Ziai for supporting my project of producing that first edition. The present second edition, like the first, incorporates not only corrections but also rewordings that occasionally affect the contents. Also, an eighth essay has been added to the seven essays of the first edition. In the first seven essays of the second edition, I have indicated within braces the corresponding page numbers of the first edition.

In addition to reiterating my gratitude to those whose names are listed on the Acknowledgements page of the first edition, I take this opportunity to thank all those who helped me in the course of preparing the second edition. I highlight the following names: Zohreh Afshar, Mohsen Ashtiany, Christopher Dadian, Niloofar Fotouhi, John McDonald, Stephen Mitchell, Sarah Morrell, Leonard Muellner, Gregory Nagy, Joseph Nagy, Rahim Shayegan, Oktor Skjærvø, Wheeler Thackston.

I owe a special debt of thanks to Richard N. Frye, whose lifelong work on Iranian civilization has taught me how to formulate in my own work the concept of an Iranian "singer of tales" (to borrow from the title of a book by Albert Lord [2000])—a concept that comes to life in the historical example of the Parthian *gōsān* (as analyzed in an article by Mary Boyce [1957]).

Introduction

{xiii}[1] This book is a set of essays unified by the central purpose of combining comparative and internal evidence in the study of Classical Persian poetics, primarily with reference to Ferdowsi's *Shāhnāma*.

In emphasizing comparative approaches, my basic question is not only how the methods of Comparative Literature enhance our understanding of Persian literature, but also how the Persian evidence in its own right illuminates some major topics of Comparative Literature today.[2]

Among these topics are (1) convergences and divergences between oral and written traditions and (2) interactions of myth and poetics. My first book, *Poet and Hero in the Persian Book of Kings*,[3] centered on these two issues, setting off lively debate by applying the comparative methods of two scholars in particular: Albert Lord and Georges Dumézil. The present book continues that debate in applying further comparative methodology as well as further evidence from Persian poetics, primarily with reference to Ferdowsi's *Shāhnāma*. In order to provide a context for proceeding further, I will also revisit key aspects of the methods applied by Lord in his comparative studies of oral poetics[4] and those applied by Dumézil in his comparative studies of parallelisms between heroes of epic and gods of myth and ritual.[5]

{xiv} The first essay elaborates on the formulations of this central purpose and gives a general overview of recent debates concerning the applications of comparative approaches to the *Shāhnāma*.

The second essay explores the impact of Lord's classic formulation of oral poetry in *The Singer of Tales* on current *Shāhnāma* studies. It challenges the assumption that oral poetics are more "primitive" and less "sophisticated" than written poetics.

The third essay concentrates on the metaphors of "singer" and "book" in the poetics of the *Shāhnāma*, showing that Ferdowsi's interweaving of these two distinct metaphors is actually compatible with oral poetics, not just written poetics.

1. Numbers in braces indicate the pagination of the first edition of the present book.

2. For a forceful articulation of the value of Comparative Literature as an academic discipline, see Guillén 1993, which is a reworking of Guillén 1985.

3. Davidson 2013[1994].

4. Lord 2000[1960], 1986, 1991, 1995.

5. Dumézil 1968–1973. For an assessment of the importance of Dumézil's work, see Skjærvø 1997a:115, 126; 1998a:645, and 1998b. For a rigorous exploration of the methods required for the study of interactions between myth and ritual, see Jamison 1991.

The fourth essay examines conflicting approaches to the assertion of earlier prose versions corresponding to later poetic versions found in the *Shāhnāma*. Instead of assuming that the prose versions are simply the "sources" of Ferdowsi's poetry, it is argued that the corresponding poetic versions derive from independent artistic conventions that cannot be explained away merely in terms of their prosaic counterparts.

The fifth essay re-examines the epithet of Rostam, *tājbakhsh* 'crown-bestower,' in comparative terms of traditional Indo-Iranian concepts of kingship, as analyzed by Dumézil. It is argued that this epithet reflects an inherited narrative theme appropriate to Rostam in his epic role as a heroic "king-maker."

The sixth and the seventh essays consider two distinct "sub-genres" within the epic genre of the *Shāhnāma*. In the sixth, the "sub-genre" is heroic boasting, as a form of first-person praise poetry, in the narrative of Rostam's duel with Esfandiyār. In the seventh, it is women's lament, framed within the epic narrative {xv} about the mourning of Sohrāb by his mother Tahmina.

The eighth essay, new to the second edition of this book, is a revised version of my 2008 review of Kumiko Yamamoto's *Oral Background of Persian Epics*,[6] an admirably insightful piece of scholarship, but one in need of substantial revision when it comes to the author's overly narrow and less-than-current understanding and characterization of oral poetics.

At the heart of my project is the study of Classical Persian poetry for its own sake. It is precisely for the sake of this poetry that I impose no arbitrary restrictions on the applications of methodologies, comparative or otherwise, new or old. There is a great deal at stake right now in this field of study. There are some specialists who prefer to contain Persian poetics (and Iranian civilization in general) by attempting to exclude and even discredit the applications of some new approaches, especially those of Lord and Dumézil. They too, like me, may claim to be studying Persian poetry for its own sake. Unlike me, though, such specialists imply that this poetry is worthwhile only for specialists like themselves. The counter-claim of my book is that such an attitude of exclusiveness impoverishes the humanistic legacy of Persian culture and of Iranian civilization in general.

By contrast with those who seek to contain Persian poetics (and Iranian civilization in general) by attempting to exclude and even discredit the applications of some new approaches, especially those of Lord and Dumézil, I argue that such comparative methods actually enhance the study of Persian poetry.

6. Davidson 2008; Yamamoto 2003.

What is ultimately at stake, in any case, is the future of studies in Classical Persian poetry. It comes down to a basic question: does this literature, as a continuation of Iranian civilization, stand on its own as a vital contribution to humanities and even to humanity itself? As one who resolutely believes that the answer is “yes,” I firmly resist the notion that any single group of specialists, any single school of thought, can claim the authority to contain or control the methods applied to the study of this literature. The ultimate test of any methodology—comparative or otherwise—is {xvi} the results achieved.

Essay One

Preliminaries about Comparative Methodology

{1} In a 1985 article and then again at greater length in my first book, *Poet and Hero in the Persian Book of Kings*, I argued that comparative methods can be applied to enhance the study of Classical Persian poetry, using Ferdowsi's *Shāhnāma* as the primary case in point.[1] Most specialists in Persian poetics evidently agree. Among them are Dick Davis,[2] Richard N. Frye,[3] Mahmud Kianush,[4] Marta Simidchieva,[5] Prods Oktor Skjærvø,[6] and G. Michael Wickens.[7] A few critics, however, display negative reactions toward comparative approaches to Ferdowsi. A brief reexamination of such reactions will help formulate the challenges ahead.

In a more recent article,[8] I was given the opportunity not only to argue against such reactions,[9] but also to write up a "white paper" arguing for the intellectual and academic trajectory of my {2} comparative work.[10] That article of mine was indeed much more than a rebuttal: it was meant as a scholarly *apologia pro vita sua*. It applied comparative methods in arguing for the oral poetic heritage of Ferdowsi's *Shāhnāma* and rejected counterarguments based on the facile assumption that oral poetry is by nature unsophisticated and "primitive." I have now reworked that article into Essay Two of this book, which I follow up with further relevant explorations in Essays Three and Four.

1. Davidson 1985 and 2013[1994]. The book is an extension as well as a reworking of the article. On the comparative methodology of Davidson 1985, see Lord 1986:467.

2. Davis 1995a:11, who remarks about Davidson 2013[1994]: "her appendix demonstrating the oral formulaic nature of the diction of much of the *Shāhnāmeh* presents such an overwhelmingly strong case that it would have to convince even the most skeptical audience."

3. Frye 1995:129.

4. Kianush 1996:1.

5. Simidchieva 1994:329, 331.

6. Skjærvø 1994:205–207, 240.

7. Wickens 1995:528–529. Since the first edition of the present book, my perspective has continued to draw supporters. See Marzolph 2002:281–282; Shayegan 2011:297n855 and 2012:139.

8. Davidson 1998b.

9. Omidsalar 1996.

10. That paper was published by the *Journal of the American Oriental Society*, which as a policy does not accept articles that aim merely to rebut reviews. It is thus significant in and of itself that it published my paper as a lead article in its Brief Communications section.

Here in Essay One, I offer some background by summarizing the comparative methods that I apply in Essays Two through Four, and by briefly tracing the history of this methodology. In my summary and in the book as a whole, we will see that the work of Albert Lord is central.

Essay Five introduces the comparative methods of another scholar whose work is also central to this book, Georges Dumézil. It is easiest to explain the combined relevance of Lord's and of Dumézil's work by now turning to another type of negative reaction facing comparative research in the study of Classical Persian poetry. I have in mind a brief review in which the writer objects to my reliance on the research of "certain earlier writers," mentioning by name Dumézil, L. P. Elwell-Sutton, Lord, and Milman Parry (he lists them in that order), and adding that he is {3} opposed to "replacing rational argumentation by name dropping."[11] In the same breath, in his very next sentence, this writer dismisses my own argumentation about the Indo-Iranian god Apām Napāt simply by referring to a "good synthesis" by Mary Boyce.[12]

Questions of "name-dropping" aside, this writer's contention about Apām Napāt will become a most useful point of entry for explaining in depth the methods and results of Dumézil in Essay Five of the present book, which offers new evidence concerning the poetic heritage of Apām Napāt and about the mythical connections of this divine construct with the heroic figure of Rostam. Here in Essay One, I confine myself to signaling the fundamentally comparative nature of Dumézil's methodology, which I connect with the comparative methods of Lord and of his teacher, Milman Parry.

As for the important comparative work on Classical Persian meters by Elwell-Sutton, mentioned *en passant* in our reviewer's list of proscribed names not to be "name-dropped," I can formulate in this single sentence the relevance of his 1976 book: in brief, the argumentation of my first book meshes with Elwell-Sutton's thesis that the meter of Ferdowsi's *Shāhnāma*, the *mutaqārib*, was derived from Iranian oral poetic traditions, not from Arab literary traditions.[13]

11. Blois 1998, a review of Davidson 2013[1994].

12. Blois 1998. Boyce's study of Apām Napāt is examined further below.

13. Elwell-Sutton 1976. Blois 2004[1992–1997]:1.49–53 attempts to discredit this argument. He thinks that the traditional Iranian meters, going all the way back to the Gāthas, "conform to a system of accentual metre" (p. 44). While he says at first that this claim of his is "a minority view" (p. 42) "to which the present author inclines" (p. 44), he says seven pages later: "In fact, as has already been mentioned, a very strong case for an accentual basis of Middle-Iranian poetry has been made by such experts as Henning and Boyce" (p. 49). This "strong case" is reported merely by way of a passing reference (p. 45) to the views of Henning (1942:52–56; 1950) and Boyce (1954, esp. pp. 45–59): "The same accentual principle underlies, according to the penetrating analyses of Henning and Boyce, pre-Islamic Middle-Persian and Parthian po-

{4} Aside from serving as convenient points of entry for my further applications of comparative methodology, the criticisms that I have read so far from those few reviewers who object to such applications tend to be of little use or novelty.[14] Moving from negative to positive perspectives on comparative methodology, I propose now to outline briefly the special importance of the work of Lord (following Parry) and of Dumézil for my own work on Persian poetry.

The fundamental insight of Parry and Lord concerning oral poetry is that *composition* and *performance* are aspects of the same poetic *process*. In other words, oral composition happens in the process of oral performance. Oral poetics is a matter of composition-in-performance. Parry and Lord derived this insight {5} from direct empirical observation of living oral traditions in former Yugoslavia, where Parry conducted his fieldwork in 1933–1935 with the assistance of Lord, who was then his student. The definitive work on Parry's fieldwork is Lord's book, *The Singer of Tales*, which was first published in 1960. After Parry's premature death in 1935, Lord continued the work of his teacher, conducting his own fieldwork in former Yugoslavia after World War II, especially in 1950–1951.[15]

In the wake of Lord's *Singer of Tales*, his empirical findings about the dynamics of oral poetry in the varied historical contexts of South Slavic Europe (both the Muslim and the Christian constituencies) were extended and reapplied—comparatively—to a variety of other contexts.[16] Primary among these other contexts was the Homeric poetry of ancient Greece, which had

---

etry." By contrast, I follow Elwell-Sutton 1976 (esp. pp. 181–182, with reference to Henning; cf. p. 170, with reference to Henning and Boyce) in resisting the idea of a proto-Iranian "system of accentual metre." Elwell-Sutton says about Persian meter (p. 75): "It is probable that the question of stress does not arise at all."

14. Besides Blois 1998, see also Herrmann 1997, whom Blois recommends to his readers for a "severe review" of my work. The main substance of Herrmann's two-page notice is that he recommends pp. 53–58 of the first fascicule of the first edition of Blois 2004[1992–1997] (= pp. 52–56 in the second edition) for a refutation of my work on "oral poetry," along with Alishan 1989 for a refutation of my work on the poetic heritage of the epic figure Rostam. Blois too (1998:269) recommends his earlier work, as well as Alishan, for a refutation of my work on "oral poetry," and now in the second edition of Blois 2004[1992–1997] (p. 56) the author recommends Herrmann 1997, Omidsalar 1996 and his own 1998 review. According to Herrmann, my efforts "have been refuted with such convincing arguments" by Blois and Alishan that "nothing important remains to be added" to these arguments ("mit so überzeugenden Argumenten zurückgewiesen worden, daß ihnen nichts Wesentliches hinzuzufügen bleibt"). The logic at work here is that of a vicious circle. In order to back up their claims, Herrmann and Blois simply cross-refer to each other, each adding Alishan for good measure.

15. For further historical background on the fieldwork of Parry and Lord, see Mitchell and Nagy's introduction to the second edition of Lord 2000[1960] (pp.vii–xxix).

16. For a survey, see Lord 1986.

originally given Parry the impetus for seeking to study comparanda in surviving traditions of living oral poetry.[17] It has often gone unnoticed that Parry's own initial work on Homeric poetry did not have the benefit of such active comparison with the living traditions of South Slavic oral poetry, nor did he live long enough to publish any of his incipient work involving direct comparisons between his research on the Homeric texts and his research on the oral traditions that he recorded later on in former Yugoslavia.[18] After Parry's death in {6} 1935, that task of comparison was left to Lord, whose 1960 *Singer of Tales* already shows a great deal of rethinking about the Homeric text—on the basis of comparative evidence collected from fieldwork in the living traditions. Chapters 7 through 9 of *Singer of Tales* are in fact concerned exclusively with Homer.[19]

Besides Homer, Lord's *Singer of Tales* chooses medieval European epic traditions as its other major point of comparison with the living oral poetry of South Slavic traditions. The text of *Singer of Tales* concluded with Chapter 10, "Some Notes on Medieval Epic."[20]

Since the original publication of *Singer of Tales* in 1960, ethnographic studies of living oral traditions all over the world have proliferated exponentially.[21] Thus the available comparanda for the original points of application, the Homeric and medieval European epic poetry, have likewise increased exponentially, as Lord himself stresses consistently in his publications since 1960.[22] And yet, ironically, most critics in the fields of classical and medieval studies confine themselves to Lord's 1960 book and to the South Slavic evidence that they find there when they debate the usefulness of comparing the recorded evidence of living oral poetry with the written evidence of ancient Greek and medieval European poetry; {7} Lord himself has noted the potential for futility in such debates, citing specific examples.[23]

A major stumbling block for these Classicist and medievalist critics is the

17. For an overview of he impact of Parry and Lord on Homeric studies see Nagy 1996a:13–27.

18. Parry 1928a (translated in Parry 1971:1–190), 1928b (translated in Parry 1971:191–239), 1930 (translated in Parry 1971:266–324) and 1932 (translated in Parry 1971:325–364). On the "Nachlass" of Milman Parry, see Mitchell and Nagy's introduction to the second edition of Lord 2000[1960].

19. Lord 2000[1960]:141–197.

20. Lord 2000[1960]:198–221.

21. For an overview of the vast influence of Lord's *Singer of Tales* on the ongoing ethnographic studies of literally hundreds of living oral traditions, see Mitchell and Nagy's introduction to the second edition of Lord 2000[1960]. For examples, I single out Blackburn 1989, Feld 1990, Okpewho 1979, Reichl 1992 and 2000, Reynolds 1995, Slymovics 1987.

22. For example: Lord 1986, 1991, 1995.

23. See especially Lord 1995:187–211.

fact that the evidence of Homeric and medieval European poetry is of course textual, whereas the evidence of recordings of living oral poetry is performative, generated by the dynamics of recomposition-in-performance.

And yet, as I argued extensively in my first book, even textual evidence can provide insights into performativity. In particular, I adduced Paul Zumthor's model of *mouvance*, which has been successfully applied to a variety of medieval European literatures.[24] This model, which my work reapplied to medieval Persian literature, helps explain the variation inherent in the *Shāhnāma* textual tradition as a symptom of ongoing recomposition-in-performance.[25]

More fundamentally, both my previous work and the present book rely on the actual language of Ferdowsi's poetry as internal evidence for formulaic composition, which can be shown to be typical of oral poetry on the basis of comparative evidence collected from recordings of living traditions. Also, the formulaic behavior of Ferdowsi's poetic diction can be connected with the thematic behavior of his poetic composition. Again, Lord's *Singer of Tales* provides a model for analyzing the functional interweaving between formula and theme, especially in Chapters 3 ("The {8} Formula") and 4 ("The Theme").[26] Essays Two through Four elaborate on this central point.

The interweaving of formula and theme in the process of recomposition-in-performance raises larger questions about the overall poetic agenda of Ferdowsi's *Shāhnāma*. Such questions cannot be addressed without an understanding of the traditional poetic genre or genres that he has inherited. Here is where I seek the central relevance of Dumézil's methods to my work. Although Dumézil does not directly address questions of formula and theme, his overall work has a direct bearing on questions of traditional genre. In order to understand the narratives about kings and heroes in *Shāhnāma*, I have found it essential to compare various cognate narratives about kings and heroes in the poetic traditions of other languages, which are cognate with Persian.

In the course of engaging in such comparisons of cognate poetic systems, we confront a most basic problem inherent in the poetic form that we are accustomed to call "epic": what is the relationship between the heroic and the divine? The key, as we will see especially in Essay Five, is Dumézil's

24. Zumthor 1972:40–41, 65–75, 507.

25. We may compare evidence from the Sasanian period of Iran indicating that "the professional storyteller ... was forbidden ever to repeat himself unless at the king's command" (Boyce 1957:34). Thus "each performance literally required a recomposition of the material" (Skjærvø 1994:207, with reference to Nagy 1990a:40).

26. Lord 2000[1960]:30–67, 68–98.

comparative approach to epic, which raises important new questions about the definition of epic as a genre. Essays Six and Seven extend these questions by re-applying Lord's comparative approach to genres beyond epic, such as men's boasting and women's lament.

Essay Two

The Text of Ferdowsi's *Shāhnāma* and the Burden of the Past[1]

{9} A review article of my first book, *Poet and Hero in the Persian Book of Kings*,[2] describes it as an "oral-formulaic study" and argues against "the relevance of Parry's and Lord's theory to the study of Persian epic literature."[3] The writer's text (I hereafter refer to both writer and text as O.) makes a variety of negative points concerning this book of mine (hereafter D.), some of which are based on misreadings.[4] I limit myself here to highlighting those of the mistakes in O. that pertain to my own positive argumentation in this essay. In the process of {10} making my arguments, I hope to develop this overall thesis: that the textual tradition of Ferdowsi's *Shāhnāma*, by way of its variant readings, reflects an oral tradition of formulaic composition.[5]

1. The title of this essay, identical to that of its precursor, Davidson 1998b, takes its inspiration from that of W. Jackson Bate's book, *The Burden of the Past and the English Poet.*

2. Davidson 2013[1994].

3. Omidsalar 1996:235; the basic works are Parry 1971 and Lord 2000[1960], 1991, 1995. Since the publication of his 1996 article, Omidsalar has continued to criticize my work in a similar vein. See Omidsalar 2002: 264, 265, 269, 270–271, 281 and 2011:200n27, 230n7. More recently, some others have also made similar arguments in opposition to my work. See for example Rubanovich 2011:654–657. With respect to the manner in which Omidsalar uses the word "theory," see Nagy 1996a:19–20: "It is a major misunderstanding ... to speak of "the oral theory" of Milman Parry and Albert Lord. Parry and Lord had investigated the *empirical reality* of oral poetry, as ascertained from the living traditions of South Slavic oral poetry as well as other living traditions. The existence of oral poetry is a fact, ascertained by way of fieldwork." The word "theory" is appropriate only in contexts where we apply to a given textual tradition what we already know inductively about oral traditions.

4. To cite just one of many available examples: the point of my argument at D. p. 3 is not, as is claimed at O. p. 236, that "Rustam is not an outsider to the epic." I argue that Rostam is an insider to the "book of kings" tradition, not only to the epic tradition. I disagree with the view that this hero is an insider only to the epic tradition. O. adduces the argument of Ṣafā 1984[1944]:564–565 that Rostam is not intrusive in the Persian epic tradition. O. misses the point: there is general agreement that Rostam in not intrusive in epic, but there is disagreement over whether he is intrusive in the book of kings tradition and whether this tradition should be considered distinct from epic. D. disagrees with Ṣafā about the status of Rostam in the book of kings tradition, not in epic.

5. As I will argue, reflexes of an oral poetic tradition can be established on the basis of *textual* evidence. See also Skjærvø 1994:205–207.

In the Appendix of D., I tested an earlier version of this thesis on a randomly-selected passage from the *Shāhnāma*, finding that "every word in this passage can be generated on the basis of parallel phraseology expressing parallel themes"[6] and that "the degree of regularity and economy in the arrangement of phraseology is clearly suggestive of formulaic language."[7] More important for the moment, I found that "the variations between variant lines in different manuscripts correspond to those between variant lines in different passages."[8] In other words, the variant readings of different manuscripts of Ferdowsi's *Shāhnāma* result from a system of formulaic variation typical of oral poetics.

The comparative method offers criteria for establishing what is or is not typical of oral poetics. There are two levels of comparison. One involves the evidence of living traditions of oral poetics as observed and described in fieldwork. The primary case in point is Parry's and Lord's research in South Slavic heroic song.[9] Another level involves the evidence of texts revealing patterns of formulaic {11} composition that are demonstrably analogous to what is observable in living oral traditions. In my own work on Classical Persian poetry, my primary point of comparison was Classical Arabic poetry, as analyzed by Michael Zwettler.[10] For Zwettler, the high degree of variation in the variant readings of any given sample textual tradition in Arabic poetry reveals the underlying system of an oral tradition: "nowhere does the inherent instability or, better, fluidity of the early Arabic poem—its essential multiformity—emerge with greater clarity than through consideration of the body of those *lectiones variae* that the textual tradition has preserved."[11] Equally important, Zwettler shows that scribal mistakes "do not constitute a major source of variation."[12]

In oral poetics, as the empirical fieldwork of Parry and Lord had shown, the burden of the poetic past becomes in varying degrees re-created with every recomposition-in-performance: variation is a primary mark of recomposition-in-performance, and Zwettler applies this discovery of Parry and Lord to Classical Arabic poetry, describing it as "a poetry that lives through variants."[13] In other words, the *variae lectiones* in the Arabic textual evidence

6. D. p. 55.

7. D. p. 55. I quote again from Davis 1995a:11: "her appendix demonstrating the oral formulaic nature of the diction of much of the *Shāhnāmeh* presents such an overwhelmingly strong case that it would have to convince even the most skeptical audience."

8. D. p. 155.

9. The best overview remains Lord 2000[1960].

10. D. pp. 55–56, with reference to Zwettler 1978.

11. Zwettler 1978:206.

12. Zwettler 1978:206.

13. Zwettler 1978:189.

can be seen as a reflex of the formulaic variants in what was formerly a living oral tradition.

O. obscures the fact that I use the evidence of Classical Arabic textual traditions {12} as a primary point of comparison with the Classical Persian. Instead, he highlights for criticism the fact that I adduce, as other points of comparison, evidence from medieval Irish and French textual traditions, as also from ancient Greek: O. claims that "a mass of irrelevant studies on Greek, Irish, and French epics crowd her references."[14] O. prefers to compare Ferdowsi to Shakespeare, Milton, and Joyce.[15] We are also told that, "unlike Homer and the Serbo-Croatian bards of Parry's and Lord's acquaintance, who practiced their art in the context of an 'oral culture,' Ferdowsi composed self-consciously, and formally, in the context of a highly literate society."[16] After all, "Khurasān of Ferdowsi's time was a hub of cultural and intellectual activity, not some backwater haven of oral tradition."[17] The city of Ṭōs in Khorasān province "was an urban center, and no matter where in the environs of the city Ferdowsi lived, he was a sophisticated urbanite, not a provincial bard."[18]

Besides making unfounded assumptions about oral poetry as something by nature unsophisticated and necessarily non-urban, O. ignores, as points of comparison, such documented cases of "sophisticated urbanites" as we find in medieval French poetic traditions. In this context I turn to my citation of one of those "irrelevant studies" criticized by O.[19] The work in question is Rupert Pickens' edition of the medieval *troubadour* songs of Jaufré Rudel {13} (*floruit* 12th century CE).[20] Pickens' editorial work is pertinent to my main thesis concerning textual variation as a symptom of compositional variation. Pickens proves that most of the textual variations in the songs of Jaufré Rudel, that is, most of the different readings transmitted by the different manuscripts, are part of a compositional system that goes beyond any individual composer. Some of the variations in the manuscript tradition of Jaufré Rudel may be due to Jaufré himself, while others are due to the transmitters of his songs in the song culture of the *troubadours*. But the point is, both kinds of variations are part of one system:

> The difference is that the modern editor and critic might consider Jaufré's changes to be "authentic," because authorized by him,

14. O. p. 236.
15. O. pp. 241–242.
16. O. p. 242.
17. O. p. 241.
18. O. p. 241.
19. D. p. 56n50.
20. Pickens 1978.

> and the transmitters' to be intrusive and destructive, despite the latters' positive motivation. Certainly, as we know by observing the manuscript tradition, authenticity was not a concern of the transmitters; moreover, Jaufré himself affirms the principle of change as esthetically proper to his genre, so that it might be said that *mouvance* is an aspect of the intention of his songs.[21]

The concept of *mouvance*, as Pickens is using it here, was formulated by the medievalist Paul Zumthor: according to this formulation, medieval texts that derive from oral traditions are not a finished product, *un achèvement*, but a text in progress, *un texte en train de se faire*.[22] No matter how many times a text derived from oral traditions is written down, it will change or *move*: hence the term *mouvance*.

{14} Following both Zumthor and Pickens, Gregory Nagy has applied the concept of *mouvance* to the history of the ancient Greek Homeric text: both the papyrus fragments (from the Hellenistic and Roman periods) and the medieval manuscripts of the Homeric *Iliad* and *Odyssey* preserve a number of variant readings that are demonstrably authentic from the standpoint of the formulaic system that generates Homeric diction.[23] In any given case where two or more authenticated variant readings are attested, Nagy argues that the editor's task is to establish which variant was used at which historical point in the evolution of the text, not to guess which is "superior" and which is "inferior":

> The empirical methods of comparative philology and the study of oral tradition can be used to defend a variant reading as traditional, not as superior. On the basis of comparative studies of textual variation in manuscript traditions that are based on oral traditions, these same empirical methods can be used to defend variant readings that happen to be attested only in manuscripts judged inferior by editors ancient or modern.[24]

In other words, to paraphrase the dictum of the great Italian philologist and humanist Giorgio Pasquali, what is *lectio difficilior* for one period in the history of a text may be *lectio facilior* for another.[25] Pasquali's insights are coincidentally but ironically pertinent to the debate at hand, since this scholar's reputation suffers the indignity of being invoked, incorrectly, by O. in his criticism of my methods in evaluating *variae lectiones*:

21. Pickens 1978:35.
22. Zumthor 1972:73.
23. Nagy 1996b, especially ch. 5; for debate, see Nagy 1997 and 1998, with bibliography.
24. Nagy 1996b:134.
25. Pasquali 1952:122; cf. Nagy 1996b:12n16, 129n99, 134n119.

> {15} Where a verse meets the procrustean requirements of her theory, she either adopts it from the critical apparatus, or from the addenda[,] and presents it as proof. When an appropriate verse is found in neither the critical apparatus nor in the addenda of the Moscow text, she reaches back to Mohl's nineteenth-century edition, and finds one there. This manner of operation is hardly expected from a scholar with some background in Classics, which, after all, is the discipline that gave us such brilliant editors as Housman, Maas, Pascuali [*sic*], Fänkel [*sic*], and many others.[26]

There are some mistaken assumptions in this statement about editorial approaches to variant readings in a given manuscript tradition, and these assumptions become evident in the specific arguments used by O. A case in point is his argumentation about the "correct spelling" of a word in the manuscript tradition of the *Shāhnāma*.[27] I will return to this specific case presently, as also to his general condemnation of the methods I use in evaluating *variae lectiones* in the *Shāhnāma*. For the moment, though, I wish to pursue further the question of determining whether a given variant reading is "superior" or "inferior," "genuine" or "spurious," even "right" or "wrong" in a given manuscript tradition.

Applying the model of *mouvance* developed by Zumthor and Pickens, Nagy writes about Homeric *variae lectiones*:

> We cannot simplistically apply the criteria of right or wrong, better or worse, original or altered, in the editorial process of sorting out the Homeric variants transmitted by Aristarchus or by earlier sources. It is indeed justifiable, however, to ask whether a variant is *authentic* or not—provided we understand "authentic" to mean *in conformity with traditional oral epic diction*. Further, it is {16} justifiable to ask whether a given variant can be assigned to a particular period.[28]

Nagy argues for the need to take all authenticated variants into account in establishing a "multitext" format for the editing of Homer: "only within such a multitext editorial framework can we turn to questions of whether one variant was more suitable than another at a given time and place."[29]

The term "multitext" derives from the work of Pickens, who has used it in reference to his 1978 edition of the songs of Jaufré Rudel: that particular edition, with its "multitext format," was "the first widely recognized edition attempting to incorporate a procedure to account for re-creative textual

26. O. p. 237.
27. O. p. 236.
28. Nagy 1996b:153.
29. Nagy 1996b:149; for further debate, with bibliography, see Nagy 1997 and 1998.

change."[30] It is this kind of editorial procedure, as I argued in D., that needs to be applied to the text tradition of the *Shāhnāma*.[31] In D., I started by comparing the textual traditions of Classical Arabic poetry as transmitted by the early editors of the texts, who evidently participated in the poetic tradition that was being transmitted: following Zwettler, I stressed that "the editors' quest for authenticity by way of examining and collecting all variants was due not so much to any need of determining the author but to the desire of {17} recovering the authentic poetic tradition of Bedouin poetry."[32] I also stressed an essential difference between the Arabic and Persian textual evidence:

> In the case of the Arabic evidence, the variants seem to have been collected *while* the given poem was evolving into a fixed text in the process of continual performance/recomposition. In the case of the *Shāhnāma*, on the other hand, the variants seem to have gone on accumulating even *after* the composition had become a fixed text by way of writing.[33]

Pursuing this distinction, I argued that oral transmission of poetry as found in the *Shāhnāma* continued side by side with the written transmission of the text. Each new occasion for performing any part of this poetry could have entailed some degree of recomposition, so that oral poetry could even influence the transmission of the text.[34] This argument affects our assumptions about the "original" text:

> This means that we cannot reconstruct with any absolute certainty the original composition of Ferdowsi, because of its susceptibility to recomposition with each new performance [of any of its parts] in a living oral tradition. All we can say about the original is that, if it is capable of being recomposed, it too must be a product of oral composition. And the continual recomposition on the level of form was matched by recomposition on the level of content, leading to new accretions that are anachronistic to the patterns of earlier layers.[35]

{18} As Theodor Nöldeke concedes, the textual transmission of the *Shāhnāma* of Ferdowsi is full of "various genuine versions" of given passages.[36] For Nöldeke, there is no "final touch" for the *Shāhnāma*.[37] As if to console himself, Nöldeke adds: "We are not really worse off than with the text of

30. Pickens 1994; the quotation is taken from p. 61; cf. Nagy 1996b:26.
31. D. pp. 56–57, citing in n50 the methodology outlined by Pickens.
32. D. p. 56, following Zwettler 1978:203.
33. D. p. 57.
34. D. pp. 57.
35. D. pp. 57.
36. Nöldeke 1930:125.
37. Nöldeke 1930:126.

Homer."[38] The Homeric analogy, as introduced by Nöldeke, was developed in my book as a way to help understand "the factor of performance in the constitution of the text of any poetry that is built on an oral tradition."[39] By contrast with Nöldeke, O. dismisses all comparisons with Homeric textual tradition, adding that the "whole corpus of Albert Lord, Millman [*sic*] Parry, and studies of the [*sic*] pre-Islamic Arabic poetry are completely irrelevant" to the Persian evidence.[40]

When he so desires, however, O. invokes his own Homeric analogies: "I may remind the reader that, unlike Homer, whose warriors frequently fall with their armor 'clattering about them,' Ferdowsi uses a stunning array of well-thought-out images for his descriptions of death in battle."[41] The reader's confidence in O.'s Homeric reminders is easily shaken, since O.'s intent to illustrate Homeric monotony has here led him to choose, inadvertently, a {19} classic example of virtuosity in Homeric variation. I refer the reader to Leonard Muellner's formulaic analysis of the celebrated Homeric expression δούπησεν δὲ πεσών, ἀράβησε δὲ τεύχε' ἐπ' αὐτῷ "he fell with a thud, and his armor clattered about him": the line-formula occurs seven times in the *Iliad* (4.504, 5.42, 5.540, 13.187, 15.578, 17.50, 17.311), and its pre-caesura segment ("he fell with a thud") is also attested "with a different half-line following it nine other times, and *each* of the nine times the second half of the line is different."[42] Muellner, commenting on this prime example of the "variation esthetic" in Homer, notes that "it is hard to imagine a literate poet creating so many expressions for a single idea," and that "only a poet equipped with a traditional language has the means or desire to carry off such a display."[43]

Here I return to my basic argument about *variae lectiones* in the *Shāhnāma*: as in the case of Homeric *variae lectiones*, we cannot mechanically apply the criteria of right or wrong, better or worse, original or altered, in the process of establishing an edition. What we can do is to establish criteria to determine which particular variant is more appropriate to which particular period in the history of the textual transmission. Such criteria require a multitext editorial procedure, as I argued in D. with reference to the methodology of Rupert Pickens.[44] I stress that such a procedure cannot be used to recover the "original":

38. Nöldeke 1930:127.
39. D. pp. 58–59.
40. O. p. 242. This kind of statement suggests a general attitude of hostility toward Comparative Literature as an academic discipline. On the humanistic value of this discipline, see in general Guillén 1993, which is a reworking of Guillén 1985.
41. O. p. 242.
42. Muellner 1976:25–6.
43. Muellner 1976:25n19.
44. D. pp. 56n50.

> {20} The archetypal fixed text of Ferdowsi's *Shāhnāma* can never be recreated, since it would be impossible to decide in any given instance which of, say, two "genuine" variants was actually composed by Ferdowsi. To understand the full creative range of the *Shāhnāma* tradition, it would be more important to have an edition that lists all variants.[45]

In this context, D. pointed to the then newly begun and still in-progress edition of the *Shāhnāma* by Djalal Khaleghi-Motlagh, and to the comments of Ehsan Yarshater, published in the introduction to the first volume, about the methodology used in this edition.[46] When I cited Yarshater's introduction, I had especially these words of his in mind:

> To guard against possible subjectivity in the selection of words or verses and to preserve the right of judgment for the reader, a critical editor of the Shahnameh ought to record and present conscientiously all the meaningful variants to the reader. Only an edition conforming to these principles may claim to be truly critical.[47]

Khaleghi-Motlagh "has selected fifteen manuscripts in order to serve the edition of the text," the variant readings of which he {21} tracks in his *apparatus criticus*.[48] To that extent, his edition comes closest so far to the desideratum of what I have described as a multitext edition. Khaleghi-Motlagh's edition still falls far short of a total accounting of *variae lectiones* (the fifteen manuscripts are chosen out of a larger collection of forty-five), but it is by far preferable to the earlier Moscow edition of Y. E. Bertels and his colleagues.[49] D. was critical of the methodology used by the Moscow editors, whose text was based on the working assumption that there must be a single correct and original reading to be recovered from amidst a plethora of variants.[50] As I argued, "if indeed textual variants arise from the perpetuation of the *Shāhnāma* in performance, we need just the opposite of the so-called critical Moscow edition."[51]

Still, D.'s citation-system of the *Shāhnāma* was keyed not to the newer edition of Khaleghi-Motlagh but to the older one of Bertels and his associates. There were two practical reasons for this choice. First, my original research on the formulaic diction of the *Shāhnāma* was published in 1988, be-

45. D. p. 60.
46. D. p. 60n63; Yarshater in Khaleghi-Motlagh 1988–2008:1.v–xi.
47. Yarshater in Khaleghi-Motlagh 1988–2008:1.x; emphasis mine.
48. Yarshater in Khaleghi-Motlagh 1988–2008:1.x.
49. Bertels *et al.*, 1960–1971.
50. D. pp. 60–62.
51. D. p. 60.

fore I could have benefited even from the first volume of Khaleghi-Motlagh, which appeared in the course of that same year.[52] In this research I needed, for methodological reasons, an entire corpus of the *Shāhnāma* for testing the sample passage that I had selected, since my goal was to show "that every word in this given passage can be generated on the {22} basis of parallel phraseology expressing parallel themes."[53] When I incorporated my earlier research into what became D., my framework of reference continued to require an entire corpus for points of formulaic comparison, and therefore I kept my citation system keyed into the completed edition of Bertels rather than the incomplete one of Khaleghi-Motlagh.

What the argumentation of O. obscures is the fact that my citation system treats the Moscow edition as a storehouse of variants, not as an absolute text. Also, I make it clear in D. that I prefer the newer edition of Khaleghi-Motlagh to the older one of Bertels.[54] Still, I reject the formulation and the underlying assumptions of O. when he says about the Khaleghi-Motlagh edition: "failure to utilize this reliable text, and relying instead on the readings of the Moscow edition, often result in serious errors of analysis."[55] The wording of O. is erroneous and misleading: the "readings of the Moscow edition" are readings of the manuscript tradition of the *Shāhnāma*, as sorted out by the Moscow editors. They are not, as O. implies, made up by the editors. Confronted with two or more variant manuscript readings, the Moscow editors will choose one of them as the "right" one and reject the others as "wrong." The basic method of the Khaleghi-Motlagh edition is no different, only much more thorough. And the basic results, built on the assumption that there can only be one right reading, can be just as tentative, despite O.'s claims about the absolute rightness of the Khaleghi-Motlagh text.

{23} A case in point is O.'s discussion of the variant readings *khān* and *khwān*, which O. considers two distinct words that are "homophones."[56] In using the word "homophone," O. implies that both spellings reflect a single pronunciation in the poetic diction of Ferdowsi, that is, *khān*.

O. recognizes that the two words had once been distinct, with separate etymologies that we may define short-hand as 'course' in the case of *khwān* and 'station' in the case of *khān*. The problem is, O.'s assertion that *khān* and *khwān* were "homophones" in the era of Ferdowsi is merely an assumption.

52. Davidson 1988. Reworked in the appendix of D. (pp. 151–160).

53. D. p. 55. For a direct application, to a large textual corpus, of Parry's methods of formulaic analysis, see Sale 1993.

54. D. pp. 60n63, 62n71, with references also to the introduction of Yarshater to the first volume of Khaleghi-Motlagh 1988–2008.

55. O. p. 237.

56. O. p. 236.

It can be counter-argued on the basis of the orthographic variations of *khw* and *kh* in the manuscripts of the *Shāhnāma* that *khw* and *kh* had been phonemically distinct in the earlier stages of the language as recorded by the scribal tradition. After *khw* and *kh* did indeed merge into *kh* at later stages of the language, this merger could indeed be reflected by scribal confusions of spelling in the manuscripts.

In contexts where we find the compound *haftkh(w)ān*, O. accepts the variant reading *khān* that is printed by Khaleghi-Motlagh as the "correct" form by contrast with the variant manuscript reading *khwān*, as printed by the Moscow editors in such contexts. In D., however, I showed that the use of the compound *haftkh(w)ān* in the *Shāhnāma* reflects a traditional poetic wordplay associating the heroic themes of fighting and feasting.[57] That is, the semantic world of heroic ordeals, as reflected by *khān* in the sense of "station," is poetically linked with the semantic world of heroic feasts, as {24} reflected by the rhyming word *khwān* in the sense of "feast," which is the stylized context for the narration of heroic ordeals.

Thus I think that O. misses the point when he claims that *khwān* and *khān* "are neither related nor are they more than mere homophones."[58] In the poetics of the *Shāhnāma*, the thematic interplay between the rhyming words *khwān* and *khān* indicates that, yes, they are indeed related—not etymologically but thematically. And yes, they are more than "mere homophones": in the poetics of the *Shāhnāma*, it is the distinctness of the two words that makes possible the thematic interplay between feasting and fighting.

O. misses the point when he claims that Khaleghi-Motlagh gives the "correct spelling" of *khān* in contexts of *haftkh(w)ān* where the Moscow edition prints *khwān*.[59] O. bases his criterion of correctness on the etymology of *khān*, ignoring the poetics of the functional interplay between *khwān* and *khān*. In this case, I would argue that the variant reading preferred by the Khaleghi-Motlagh edition is "less correct" than the one preferred *passim* by the Moscow edition.[60] I place "less correct" in quotation marks, because this criterion can be applied only historically—in this case from the standpoint of an era in the ongoing poetics of the *Shāhnāma* that predates the phonemic merger of *khw* and *kh*.

In general, O. needs to be corrected wherever he implies that I simply follow the Moscow edition's readings. What I report in D. when I use the Moscow edition are the variant readings {25} of the manuscripts as reported in turn by the Moscow editors, and I report them without regard for wheth-

57. D. p. 139–140.
58. O. p. 236.
59. O. p. 236.
60. Bertels *et al.* 1960–1971:6.167.25–26, as cited in D. p. 140–141.

er they happen to be chosen by the editors as the true reading, to be placed in the text proper, or whether they are rejected as a false reading, to be relegated to the *apparatus criticus* or to the "addenda." It is simply wrong for O. to claim that I have "continued to rely on the outdated and seriously flawed readings of the Moscow edition."[61] In fact, we have already seen another claim of his that actually contradicts this one, concerning my selective use of *variae lectiones* as reported in the Moscow edition: "Where a verse meets the procrustean requirements of her theory, she either adopts it from the critical apparatus, or from the addenda[,] and presents it as proof."[62] It seems that O. wants to have it both ways: he criticizes me for citing variants that are deemed correct by the Moscow editors, but he also criticizes me for citing variants that they deem incorrect. By his criteria, the only correct variant is whatever is printed in the main text of the edition by Khaleghi-Motlagh.

O.'s dogmatism in claiming absolute correctness for the edition of Khaleghi-Motlagh is in fact a violation of the spirit of scholarly inquiry encouraged by the format of Professor Khaleghi-Motlagh's editorial work, which makes his edition superior to the others. Here I must repeat the essential words of Ehsan Yarshater in his introduction to the first volume of this edition: "To guard against possible subjectivity in the selection of words or verses and to preserve the right of judgment for the reader, a critical editor of the {26} Shahnameh ought to record and present conscientiously all the meaningful variants to the reader."[63] It seems to me that my methodology, in seeking to evaluate the relative merits of all *variae lectiones* in the *Shāhnāma* tradition, promotes the scholarly imperative of Yarshater's formulation. And it also seems to me that O.'s approach, in rejecting my methods, promotes the opposite: that is, he seeks to deny the right of judgment to the reader.

In an article reviewing the third volume of Khaleghi-Motlagh's edition of the *Shāhnāma*, Dick Davis has singled out for praise the editor's policy of tracking the *variae lectiones* in a clearly-formatted apparatus.[64] Surveying questions of major textual variation in the manuscript traditions, especially in the case of the Florence manuscript, Davis views the new cumulative evidence of the variants collected by Khaleghi-Motlagh as a vindication of my central argument concerning variation as a symptom of formulaic diction:

> One of the great virtues of the present edition is that its apparatus

61. O. p. 237.
62. O. p. 237.
63. Yarshater in Khaleghi-Motlagh 1988–2008:1.x; emphasis mine.
64. Davis 1995b.

> brings such questions [of variation] into the open and makes them relatively easy to debate, but it also indicates that the text of the *Shahnameh* seems in many places to be even more unstable than might have been feared. So much so that Olga Davidson's recent suggestion (in *Poet and Hero in the Persian Book of Kings* ... pp. 65–72 [= 56–62 in the third edition]) that the text of Ferdowsi's poem may have remained in a state of some flux, due to oral performance, for some time after its first "publication" (and that to search for an ur-text is thus to set off after an ignis fatuus) becomes particularly attractive. The discovery of the Florence manuscript has not in fact solved many issues as much as it has opened up some new ones.[65]

{27} In a separate article, Davis has put together a set of powerful arguments in favor of positing, as I do, an oral poetic tradition as the foundation of Ferdowsi's *Shāhnāma*.[66] Davis agrees with my argument that such a tradition is reflected in Ferdowsi's stylized references—not only to performances of passages from the Book of Kings tradition but also to an archetypal Book of Kings that had been once upon a time lost or scattered, only to become reintegrated as the ultimate "source" of Ferdowsi's own monumental composition.[67]

I will have more to say in Essay Three about this important article of Davis. Suffice it for now to observe that it answers, albeit indirectly, many of the negative arguments directed by O. against my book.[68] Here I have offered my own answers only to the extent of defending D. and thereby advancing further my positive argument that variant readings of the *Shāhnāma* reflect the heritage of an oral poetic tradition. As for O.'s pronouncements about "right" {28} and "wrong" variants, climaxing with his catalogue of "wrong" variant readings that I have used in my citations (O. describes one such reading as "a vulgar and artless interpolated verse"), they have to be viewed in the larger context of the methodological and even logical confusion that pervades his whole article. I close with an example where O.'s confusion ex-

65. Davis 1995b:395. For more on the Florence manuscript, see D. pp. 61–62, with reference to the fundamental work of Piemontese 1980.

66. Davis 1996, with reference to D. at p. 48n1. See also p. 53n22: "Olga Davidson analyzes a randomly selected passage, showing convincingly that virtually the whole of it consists of stock formulae." See also his review, Davis 1995a, mentioned in Essay One above.

67. See Part 1 of D. (pp. 13–63), an earlier version of which was published in Davidson 1985. The relevant portions of my discussion in the earlier version can be found at pp. 103–142, where I also address the problem of the "older preface" to the *Shāhnāma*. The solution that I attempt there (further elaborated in D. pp. 24–46) matches closely the one proposed in the later article of Davis 1996.

68. For example, Davis's analysis of the usage of *pahlavi* (1996:51n12) effectively rebuts O.'s objections (p. 238) to my interpretation of the contexts of this word (D. pp. 35–36).

tends to the meaning of an English word: when I translated *sarāyanda* as "singer" in the first edition of D., I clearly meant it in the general performative sense of "singer," exactly as the word is used in the title of Albert Lord's book, *The Singer of Tales*.[69] It seems to me clear from the attestations that O. collects from the *Shāhnāma*,[70] which he intends as counter-examples to the meaning of "singer" as he narrowly understands it, that the semantic range of *sarāyanda* vindicates the meaning that Lord had intended in his title, that is, a performer of oral traditions.[71] If we grasp Lord's meaning, we may appreciate more fully the richness of variety in the Persian poetic heritage conveyed by the *Shāhnāma*.

69. I now translate *sarāyanda* as 'reciter'. Contrast pp. 36–37 of the first edition of D. with 31 of the third. I have made this change because 'singer' can be misunderstood in this context. My original translation 'singer' was meant in the sense of the title of Lord's book, *The Singer of Tales*, where 'singer', to repeat, conveys the general sense of 'performer' used in contexts of anthropological studies, not the specific sense of 'singer' as used in other contexts. When I translate *sarāyanda* as 'reciter', I continue to have in mind that same general sense of 'performer'.

70. O. pp. 240–241.

71. In the next essay, I will survey a wide variety of contexts in which this word *sarāyanda* is attested.

Essay Three

Singer of Tales and Book of Kings in the Poetic World of Ferdowsi

{29} The focus of this essay is on the word *sarāyanda* in the *Shāhnāma* of Ferdowsi, which I translated as "singer" in the first edition of *Poet and Hero in the Persian Book of Kings*.[1] As I have already noted, I meant it in the general performative sense of "singer," as the word is used in the title of Albert Lord's book, *The Singer of Tales*.[2] In the first part of this essay, I argue that the variety of contexts associated with the word *sarāyanda* in the *Shāhnāma* fits the general idea of "singer" that Lord had intended in his title, that is, a *performer* of oral poetic traditions.[3] In the second part, I will argue that the specific details of this variety of contexts reflect the attitudes of medieval Persian culture toward the overall idea of a Book of Kings.

The noun *sarāyanda* stems from the Iranian root *sru-*, the "weak" form of *srav-/srāv-*. This root is cognate with Indic *śravas-*, and its basic meaning is 'glorification' *by way of poetry/singing*.[4] The primary infinitive of the corresponding verb is *sorudan*, and the secondary infinitive is *sorāyidan*—both meaning to 'sing', 'recite', 'compose'. In the 1935 *Glossar* of Fritz Wolff, *sarāyanda* is glossed as 'Sänger', 'Dichter', while the verb *sorāyidan* (which he {30} transliterates as *sarāyidan*) is 'singen', (schön) 'reden', 'verkünden'; the verb *sorudan* is glossed as '(singen)', 'sagen', 'sprechen'.

The idea of "singing" cannot be universalized culturally, except to the extent that all singing is a matter of performance. Each culture can be expected to have its own specific traditional forms of singing. In the case of the living South Slavic traditions as studied by Lord, epic belongs to the category of "singing." There is a close analogy here with the epic traditions of

1. As I noted already in Essay 2, I now prefer to translate *sarāyanda* as 'reciter', rather than 'singer' in the general sense of 'performer'.

2. See the ending of the previous essay. For the term "performative" see especially Martin 1989 and Nagy 1996a and b.

3. In Davidson 2013a[1994]:29–34, I have studied the words *mōbad* and *dehqān* in a similar vein.

4. On the Indo-European linguistic heritage of this root, see Schmitt 1967 ch. 2; Nagy 1999a[1979]:16–18; Watkins 1995:12–13.

ancient Greece: at the beginning of the Homeric *Iliad* (1.1) for example, the Muse is invoked to "sing" (verb *aeidō*) the anger of Achilles.[5]

To be sure, even the idea of "epic" cannot be universalized, but we can see nevertheless a close analogy between the *Iliad* of Homer and the *Shāhnāma* of Ferdowsi when it comes to the heroic subject-matter of these two monumental poems. It was in this context of likening the poetry of Ferdowsi to "epic" that I drew attention in my first book to the usage of *sarāyanda* 'singer' in the *Shāhnāma,* since this word refers specifically to the medium of the {31} *Shāhnāma.*[6] That is, the medium of Ferdowsi is equated in his poem with the medium of the "singer," the *sarāyanda.* To this extent, there is a close analogy between the media of Homer and of Ferdowsi: it seems as if both were meant to be sung. To this extent, at least, it seems as if Ferdowsi were a "singer of tales."

But the realities of medieval Persian culture make it clear that this formulation cannot suffice. In my book I also drew attention to another formulation in the *Shāhnāma* about the medium of the *Shāhnāma*: this poem prominently refers to itself as a book.[7] In terms of medieval Persian culture, the medium of the singer is not incompatible with the medium of the book.[8] Here we see a major difference between Ferdowsi and the typical "singer of tales" in the South Slavic traditions studied by Lord. The South Slavic *guslar,* that is, the traditional singer who sings to the accompaniment of the string instrument called the *gusle,* practices a craft that is incompatible with literacy, as Lord showed persuasively in his *Singer of Tales.*[9]

Such incompatibility, however, should not be confused with the general term "oral poetry" that Lord used in referring to the medium of the generic Singer of Tales. The essential characteristic of oral poetry, as Lord made clear, is not that it is *not written* but that it is *performed*—that it comes to life in *performance.* The origins of oral poetry predate writing, but the essence of oral poetry does not depend on the absence of writing.[10] In his later works, especially in *Epic Singers and Oral Tradition* (1991) and *The Singer Resumes the Tale* (1995), Lord has drawn attention to emerging patterns of coexistence and even compatibility between literacy and oral poetry in various cultures, especially in medieval Europe.[11]

5. Nagy 1999b:142.
6. Davidson 2013a[1994]:30–31.
7. Davidson 2013a[1994]:16–17, 27–29, 40–46.
8. Davidson 2013a[1994]:16–17, 27–29, 40-46.
9. Lord 2000[1960]; his position has often been oversimplified and even misunderstood; for important clarifications, see Lord 1991 and 1995.
10. Lord 1995:105n26, with reference to Nagy 1990b:8.
11. See also Nagy 1996a:7–38.

Following Lord, I have stressed in my previous book the essential {32} feature of oral poetry, that is, its *performativity*. It is precisely this feature, I now argue, that we see reflected in the contexts of *sarāyanda* in the *Shāhnāma* of Ferdowsi. This is not to say that we can take as literal truth all the various references of the *Shāhnāma* to itself as the medium of the *sarāyanda*. For the moment, I interpret these self-references merely as metaphors. Still, I will go on to argue that the metaphorical world of the *Shāhnāma* reflects the real world of the poet as its performer.

Let us begin with the four contexts of *sarāyanda* that I have already quoted in my first book:[12]

1. Bertels 3.7.19–20:

بگفتار دهقان کنون باز گرد   نگر تا چه گوید سراینده مرد
چنین گفت موبد که یک روز طوس   بدانگه که بر خاست بانگ خروس

Now turn back to the words of the *dehqān*.
Consider what the *sarāyanda* says.

Thus the *mōbad* said, that, one day, Ṭōs,
at the time when the cock crowed,

As I argued at length in my first book, the voices of authoritative figures like the *dehqān* and the *mōbad* are represented as poetic sources of the *Shāhnāma*. These sources are supposed to be performative, not textual, unlike the early books of kings that the *Shāhnāma* also claims as its other main poetic source. In the present context, the roles of the *dehqān* and the *mōbad* as authoritative {33} poetic voices of the past are being equated with the role of the *sarāyanda*. The synonymity of *sarāyanda* with *dehqān* and *mōbad* in this context underlines the authority of the voice, as parallel to the authority of the book.

2. Mohl 5.424.813

سراینده دهقان موبد نژاد   ازین داستانم چنین داد یاد

A *sarāyanda*, a *dehqān* of *mōbad* descent,
from this story taught me thus.

This expression marks the introduction to the story of Shāpur Dhu'l Aktāf. I note that the authority here is expressed not in terms of synonymity but in terms of genealogy.

12. Davidson 2013a[1994]:30–31.
13. Not in Bertels.

Next, here are two more instances of synonymity:

3. Bertels 3.169.2587

بگفتار دهقان کنون باز گرد   نگرتا چه گوید سراینده مرد

Now turn back to the words of the *dehqān*.
Consider what the *sarāyanda* says.

4. Bertels 6.373.6

چه گفت آن سراینده دهقان پیر   ز گشتاسپ وز نامدار اردشیر

What did the *sarāyanda* say, that sage *dehqān*,
about Goshtāsp and famous Ardashir?

(In the last example, the rhetorical question signals the introduction {34} to an extended narrative about Dārāb.)

Now I turn to a survey of further instances of *sarāyanda* in the *Shāhnāma*, not discussed in my first book. Let us start with two straightforward cases where the *sarāyanda* is explicitly described as a court poet whose task is to glorify the kings of the past for the edification and continued glorification of the king of the present.

5. Bertels 8.151.1647/Mohl 6.300.1699

سراینده بسیار همراه کرد   به افسانه ها راه کوتاه کرد

He [= Shāh Anōshirvān] took with him several *sarāyanda*-s
to shorten the journey with stories of the past [*afsānehā*].

The context is this: the Shāh has just survived a crisis, overcoming the machinations of his own minister, the treacherous Mahbud. Later, while setting out to hunt, he is reminded of his close escape and wonders out loud about the uncertainties of life. Yearning to recover his own sense of certainty, he takes with him (*hamrāh kard*) on the hunt several *sarāyanda*-s to shorten the journey with their tales/parables/stories of past events, *afsānehā*. The entertainment provided by the *sarāyanda*-s thus has a serious purpose: it reinforces the patterns of certainty in life that the king needs in order to maintain his kingship.

6. Bertels 4.10.33–34/Mohl 2.560.39–40

دل شاه شد زان سخن شادمان   سراینده را گفت کاباد مان
که اویست پروردگار پدر   وز ویست پیدا بگیتی هنر

The heart of the Shāh rejoiced at these words.
He said to his *sarāyanda*: "May you continue to flourish,

for he [Rostam] was *parvardegār* [giver of nourishment as a foster father and mentor] to [my] father,
and from him *honar* [virtue and skill] springs into the world.

Key Khosrow is holding court, and all the nobles are assembled to pay homage to him as he begins his reign. When the heroes Rostam and Zāl enter, the Shāh turns to his *sarāyanda* and tells him what we see quoted above. The king speaks to the *sarāyanda* in the singer's capacity as a court poet, telling him to study the greatness of the hero Rostam as the stuff of great poetry.

It is clear that Ferdowsi presents himself as a continuator of such a *sarāyanda*, as we see from the following examples:

7. Bertels 2.156.457/Mohl 2.50.538

چه گفت آن سراینده مرد دلیر   که ناگه بر آویخت با نرّه شیر

What did the *sarāyanda*, the valiant man, say
when suddenly he [Rostam] tangled with a male lion?

Before Rostam's feat is narrated, the poet asks rhetorically what the *sarāyanda* said and then proceeds to "quote" the maxims of the *sarāyanda* about combat and valor. The poetic effect is to establish a direct line of continuity between the present narrator and the previous one, the stylized *sarāyanda*. This continuity is expressed {36} in terms of performance.

8. Bertels 3.6–7.2, 19/Mohl 2.194.2, 8

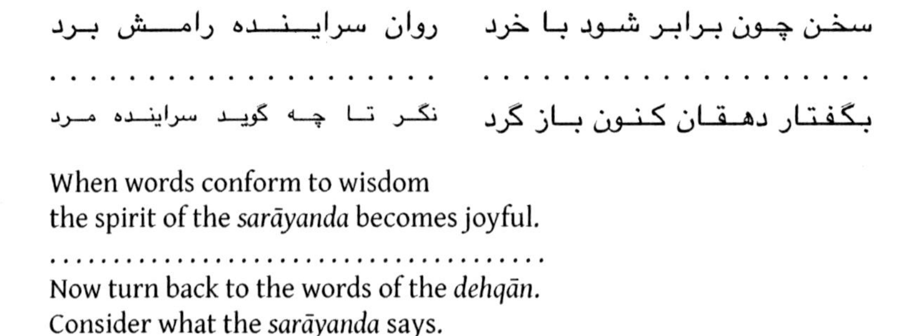

When words conform to wisdom
the spirit of the *sarāyanda* becomes joyful.

. . . .

Now turn back to the words of the *dehqān*.
Consider what the *sarāyanda* says.

The second of these two sets of distichs has already been quoted at no. 3 above. Here I add comments about the immediate context. Both sets refer to the tale of Siyāvosh, which is about to be narrated. In the context of this prelude to narration, the word *sarāyanda* is deployed twice. The first occurrence signals the poet's awareness that the story needs to be told well and wisely. The poet adds that if he does the opposite, he will be despised by his audience, who know better than to accept an inferior narration. If the composition is true and passes the scrutiny of those who know, it will then last throughout time. The performative aspect of the *sarāyanda* is highlighted by the reference to the audience's reception as the guarantor of perpetual fame.

9. Bertels 7.115.46/Mohl 5268.42

کنون ای سراینده فرتوت مرد   سوی گاه اشکانیان باز گرد

{37} Now, o *sarāyanda*, old man,
return to the enthroned time of the Ashkanians.

This expression marks a new stretch of narrative. It is as if the poet Ferdowsi had to hear the performer of the past in order to launch his own composition in the present.

10. Bertels 4.25.275/Mohl 2.582.277

چو خورشید تابان بر آمد ز کوه   سراینده آمد ز گفتن ستوه

When the sun rose, shining forth from the mountains,
and the *sarāyanda* was worn out from tale-telling [*goftan*] ...

In this context, the mention of *sarāyanda* marks the transition from night to day as Key Khosrow is about to organize his army. By implication, this point in the narrative is appropriate for the start of a new performance. The performer of the previous stretch of narrative has been worn out. A new performer is needed for the new stretch. The medium of the book can subsume both the old performer and the new performer, producing the same single poet. Ferdowsi, as the poet of the *Shāhnāma*, becomes the overall narrator of sub-narratives delimited by the endurance-levels of live performances.

11. Mohl 2.432.6, 15[14]

سراینده ز آواز بر گشت سیر   همش لحن بلبل هم آوای شیر

. . . .

بگفتار دهقان کنون باز گرد   نگر تا چه گوید سراینده مرد

14. Not in Bertels.

{38} The *sarāyanda* has grown weary of the *āvāz* [sound, clamor, fame].
The *lahn* [melody] of the nightingale and the *āvā-ye* [contract form of *āvāz*] of the lion are the same for him.

. . . .

Now turn back to the words of the *dehqān*.
Consider what the *sarāyanda* says.

These two references to the *sarāyanda* signal a shift from one sub-narrative to another—or we may say, by extension, *from one potential performance to another*. The overall narrative about the reign of Key Kāʾus continues after the sub-narrative about Siyāvosh has ended. A new sub-narrative is about to begin.

The master narrative, as framed by the Book of Kings, is pictured as transcending the endurance-levels of live performances (as signaled in the example previous to the one just mentioned). The sustained presence of the book, as a medium, transcends the pressures of live performance. In a live performance, the fatigue of the performer or of the audience can blur the distinction between the song of the nightingale and the roar of the lion. It is as if the beauty of the poetry and the terror of the subject-matter that it conveys become indistinguishable as the lengthiness of performances begins to put an undue strain on the audience's powers of concentration.

{39} 12. Bertels 8.282.3925–3926/Mohl 6.494.4041–2

چهارم که دانا دلارای خواند   سراینده را مرد با رای خواند
که پیوسته گوید سراسر سخن   اگر نو بود داستان گر کهن

Fourth, the wise man calls it desirable
and calls a *sarāyanda* a man of sound intelligence

when having connected he speaks from beginning to end a speech
whether it be a new story or an ancient one.

Here the Shāh Anōshirvān is answering a *mōbad*'s questions. He had been asked how many and what kinds of speech (*goftār*) there are. The Shāh says that wise men (*dānā*) call a *sarāyanda* someone who is of sound intelligence (*bā rāy*) and one who recites *dāstān*—whether they be old or new in speech (*sokhan*)—and who is connected (*payvasta*) from beginning to end (*sarāsar*). In other words, the *sarāyanda* is a poet whose poetry comes to life in narrating, in performing a narration, in performance.

I round out my survey of the word *sarāyanda* in the *Shāhnāma* by considering a list of examples that Omidsalar has adduced in arguing against the meaning of "singer."[15] In the previous essay, I undertook a rebuttal of this critic's general assumptions, concluding with the observation that his understanding of *sarāyanda* is too narrow.[16] Here I examine the specific examples that he adduces. In some of {40} these examples, *sarāyanda* is applied to a person who is not a professional court poet. But the point is, in each of these examples, the person in question is speaking like a *sarāyanda*. Further, in each of these examples there is a reference being made to the traditional craft of the *sarāyanda*.

13. Bertels 8.311.4404/Mohl 6.536.4544

چـه گفت آن سرایـنـدهٔ سالخورد چـو انـدرز نوشین روان یـاد کرد

What did that aged *sarāyanda* say
when he recollected the testament of Anōshirvān?

The context is this: Anōshirvān is appointing his son Hormozd as his successor. Anōshirvān's legacy is being recorded for the benefit of Hormozd, and this recording takes place in poetic form. That is, the language of the Shāh's legacy is the language of poetry, the language of the *sarāyanda*.

14a. Bertels 1.87.134

سرایـنـده جـنـدل چـو پـاسخ شنید ببوسید تختش چنان چـون سزید

Jandal the *sarāyanda*, when he heard his answer,
kissed his [Sarv's] throne as is appropriate.

14b. Bertels 1.87.144

سرایـنـده باشید و بسیار هوش بـگـفـتـار او بـر نهــاده دو گوش

{41} Be a *sarāyanda* and be very cautious,
having positioned both ears on his speech.

These two examples highlight the role of the *sarāyanda* as a court poet, one who must be a tactful communicator, by way of his poetry, in fraught situations. The Shāh Faridun sends out one of his *nāmdārān* (counselors), Jandal, as a *ferestāda* (messenger) to the King of Yemen, entrusted with the delicate task of asking the Yemeni king to give his three daughters in marriage to Faridun's three sons. The first of these two examples comes at the

15. Omidsalar 1996:240–241.
16. See also the article on which that essay was based, Davidson 1998b, especially p. 68.

exact narrative moment when Sarv, the Yemeni king, gives his answer. Then "sweet talking Jandal, when he heard the answer, kissed his [Sarv's] throne as is appropriate." In the second example, Faridun, having heard Sarv's answer from Jandal, now counsels his sons about how they should conduct themselves in Yemen, as they arrive for the purpose of winning Sarv's daughters as their wives. What makes the "sweet talk" of these negotiations and instructions really "sweet" is the fact that they are formulated through and in poetry, through and in the traditional medium of the *sarāyanda*. The diplomacy and even the charm of the poet's "sweet talk" is metonymically reassigned to the characters who get to speak the lines that have been prefabricated for them by the sweet-talking poet.[17]

15. Bertels 8.42.219/Mohl 6.142.218

قباد سراینده گفتش بگوی   بمن تازه کن در سخن آب روی

{42} Qobād the *sarāyanda* said to him "Speak
and refresh me with fluid speech."

It is the reign of Qobād, son of Piruz. Before he adopts the faith of Mazdak, Qobād has an interview with him. There is a famine, and the people had come to Qobād for relief. Mazdak intercedes for them and tells them that Qobād will take care of their problem. He then rushes to Qobād and asks him, in the form of parables, various hypothetical questions about who is responsible for human suffering. He who had the means to relieve human suffering—but did not—is not he the one who is ultimately responsible for any death incurred? Since Qobād gives a just response to these hypothetical situations of human suffering, he is answering like an able *sarāyanda*—whose precise task as court poet is to speak well, to give good answers in the form of parables.

16. Bertels 5.359.2113

تو دانی که من خود سراینده ام   پرستندهٔ آفریننده ام

You know that I myself am a *sarāyanda*
and that I am a *parastandeh* [worshipper, visionary, poet] of the Creator.

The speaker is Key Khosrow, towards the end of his life, in a private conversation with God, who sees all and can find anything. Khosrow asks God for help in finding Afrāsiyāb because he has not heard any fame (*nām*)

17. For more on the poetic device of reassigning the role of the poet to the role of the character that is being "quoted" by the poet, see Essay Six.

or rumor (*āvāz*) about him in the material world. In so many words, Khosrow says of himself that he has {43} been a good singer of hymns. In asking for "news" about Afrāsiyāb, however, he is in effect asking for even more poetic aptitude, that is, to be able to know what it is that poets sing about the deeds of Afrāsiyāb.

17. Bertels 8.248.3442

پزشک سراینده برزوی بود   بنیرو دسیده سخنگوی بود

Borzōy was a *sarāyanda* physician;
he had attained great faculty of speech.

The context is this: Borzōy brings the *Kalīla and Dimna* to Anōshirvān's library. Retrospectively, his contribution of a literary classic to Persian culture renders him a literary figure in his own right, by poetic metonymy, in this poeticized retelling of his accomplishment.[18]

18. Bertels 7.29.407

پزشک سراینده آمد بکوه   بیاورد با خویشتن زان گروه

The *sarāyanda* physician came to the mountains
and brought with him a crowd from them.

Alexander meets an Indian physician who is well known for his herbal cures. As the doctor prescribes various remedies for {44} Alexander, he simultaneously counsels the king about his morals, urging him to lead a more ascetic life. Poetry becomes metaphorized as healing, and the healer uses the words of the poet, the *sarāyanda.*[19]

As a parallel to this specific formulation, I conclude this inventory with a general formulation that applies to all the contexts that I have surveyed by now: the poetry of Ferdowsi is metaphorized as the performance of the *sarāyanda.*[20]

It is at this point that I can now turn to the second part of this essay, which will treat an equally essential metaphor at work in the *Shāhnāma*, to

18. For an attempt to reconstruct the history of this text, see Blois 1990, on which I have more to say later on in this essay.

19. On the poetic theme of the ode as "antidote," compare Pindar *Nemean* 8.49–50, and the comment of Nagy 1990b:120.

20. This inventory can be supplemented by the complementary inventory in Davidson 2013a[1994]:30–33, featuring contexts where the poetry of Ferdowsi is metaphorized as the performance of a *mōbad* or *dehqān*.

be summarized this way: the poetry of Ferdowsi is also metaphorized as the recovery of an archetypal Book of Kings.

As I have argued extensively in my earlier work, "the medium of Ferdowsi's *Shāhnāma* talks about itself both as a stylized performance and as a stylized book."[21] Furthermore, the *Shāhnāma* refers to its sources "in terms that suit either stylized performances or a stylized book."[22] My main point is that the *poetic* concept of an archetypal book as the claimed source of Ferdowsi's *Shāhnāma* is not at all incompatible with the likewise *poetic* concept of claiming {45} the actual performances of a *sarāyanda* as an authoritative source.

There are two central passages in Ferdowsi's *Shāhnāma* concerning the theme of an authoritative book as the poet's source. In my first book, I argued that both of these passages reflect the mentality of an oral poetic tradition. Here I offer merely a summary of my argumentation, referring to these two *Shāhnāma* passages short-hand as (1) the "mystical gift" and (2) the "regenerated archetype."

Let us begin with the first mention of the authoritative sourcebook, the passage about the "mystical gift." When Ferdowsi says at the opening of his monumental poem that he received an archetypal Book of Kings, written in Pahlavi, as a gift from a mysterious "friend" (1.23.156–161 Bertels), I argue that he is in effect laying claim to the authority of all previous "books of kings."[23] Such a claim, I further argue, is typical of oral traditions that coexist with written traditions:

> Ferdowsi's claimed control over both oral and written traditions ... is an expression of authority that is derived primarily from oral, not written, poetic traditions. Ferdowsi's poetic tradition was an oral tradition in its own right, and his *Shāhnāma* had survived as a living oral tradition in the period following its composition. Ferdowsi's poetry ... was an accretive medium that kept adapting itself to the society for which it was composed and recomposed.[24]

{46} A key to this argumentation is the second central passage, about the "regenerated archetype," to which we now turn. Here we see Ferdowsi's own description of the genesis of the Pahlavi book of Kings that he claims

21. Davidson 2013a[1994]:27.
22. Davidson 2013a[1994]:27.
23. Davidson 2013a[1994]:27–29, with commentary on the mystical implications of *mehrbān* 'friend'. On the convention of describing the archetypal book as written in Pahlavi, see Davidson 2013a[1994] pp. 2, 3, 5, 16, 28–29, 33, 35–39; also Davis 1996:51.
24. Davidson 2013a[1994]:24.

as his source. In this description, "we have what amounts to a myth-made stylization of oral poetry."[25] A noble and wise *pahlavān*, who is described as a hereditary *dehqān*, assembles *mōbad*-s from all over Iran, each of whom possesses a "fragment" of a preexisting Pahlavi book that had disintegrated through neglect. What now happens is an imagined reintegration of the disintegrated text. After all the *mōbad*-s are lined up in the correct order, each of them is called upon to recite his own part of the notional totality that is the Book. It is thus that this ancient but once "fragmented" Book is wondrously reassembled by the assembly of *mōbad*-s:

Bertels 1.21.126–136

یکی نامه بود از گه باستان   فراوان بدو اندرون داستان
پراکنده در دست هر موبدی   ازو بهرهٔ نزد هر بخردی
یکی پهلوان بود دهقان نژاد   دلیر و بزرگ و خردمند و راد
پژوهندهٔ روزگار نخست   گذشته سخنها همه باز جست
ز هر کشوری سالخورد   بیاورد کاین نامه را یاد کرد
بپرسیدشان از کیان جهان   وزان نامداران فرُخ مهان
که گیتی به آغاز چون داشتند   که ایدون بما خوار بگذاشتند
چه گونه سر آمد بنیک اختری   برایشان همه روز کند آوری
بگفتند پیشش یکایک مهان   سخنهای شاهان و گشت جهان
چو بشنید ازیشان سپهبد سخن   یکی نامور نامه افکند بن
چنین یادگاری شد اندر جهان   برو آفرین از کهان و مهان {47}

There was a book [*nāma*] from ancient times
in which there was an abundance of stories.

It was dispersed into the hands of every *mōbad*.
Every wise one [of the *mōbad*-s] possessed a portion of it.

There was a *pahlavān*, born of the *dehqān*-s,
brave, powerful, wise, and noble,

one who inquired into the earliest days.
He sought anew all the past stories.

From every region an aged *mōbad*
he brought, for he [the *mōbad*] remembered well this book [*nāma*].

25. Davidson 2013a[1994]:41.

He asked them about kings of the world
and about the famed and glorious heroes,

when and how they held the world in the beginning
that they should have passed it down to us in such a wretched state.

How, with a lucky star
every day completed a heroic exploit for them.

The great ones, one by one, recited before him
the stories [*sokhanhā*] about kings and the turnings of the world.

When the lord heard their words from them
he began to compose a renowned book [*nāma*].

Thus it became his memorial in the world.
The small and the great praise him.

{48} Over a century and a half ago, Jules Mohl had already interpreted this same passage as an example of a well-known type of myth that serves to explain the genesis of a national epic poetic tradition.[26] As a further example of such a myth, I have adduced a medieval French parallel, the romance known as *Guiron le courtois* (composed around 1235).[27] This romance begins with a prologue telling of a mythical Latin book about the Holy Grail, parts of which kept getting "translated" into French:

> Car bien est veritez que aucun saint homme, clerc e chevalier s'en sont ja entremis de translater ce livre de latin en langue françoise. Mesires Luces de Gau s'en entremist premierement: ce fu li premiers chevaliers qui s'estude y mist et sa cure, bien le savons; et cil translata en langue françoise partie de l'estoire mon seigneur Tristran, et mains assez que il ne deust ... Aprés s'en entremist mesires Gasses le blons, qui parens fu le roi Henri. Aprés s'en entremist maistres Gautiers Map, qui fu cleders au roy Henri et devisa cil l'estoire de mon seigneur Lancelot du Lac que d'autre chose ne parla il mie gramment en son livre. Misries Robert de Borron s'en atremist aprés.

> For it is certainly true that several holy men, clerks and knights have already undertaken to translate this book from Latin into French. Sir Luce del Gat first took it up. And he was the first knight who devoted his study and bent his will to it, as we well know. And he translated into French part of the story of Lord Tristan, and indeed less than he should have ... Next Sir Gace the Blond took it up, who was a relative of King Henry. Next Sir Walter Map took it up, who was clerk to King

26. Mohl 1838–1878:1.xi. See Davidson 2013a[1994]:43.
27. Davidson 2013a[1994]:38n43, with reference to Huot 1991:218–221.

> Henry. And he {49} worked on the story of Lord Lancelot du Lac, for he did not speak much about anything else in his book. Sir Robert de Boron took it up next.[28]

The narrative of the prologue continues up to the present time of its narrator, one Hélie de Boron; Sylvia Huot summarizes the decisive point of the narration:

> So abundant a source is this Latin Ur-text that even after all of the aforementioned translations, King Henry realizes that *ne encore n'estoit dedens tous ses livres mis ce que li livres du latin devisoit, ains en remest a translater molt grant partie* ("all his books still did not contain that which the Latin book told of, for there remained a large part of it still to translate"[29]). It is from this untranslated portion of the Latin book, of course, that *Guiron le courtois* is supposedly produced. Like the *Perceforest* author, Hélie inscribes himself in a historical movement from Latin to French literary expression. What is also clear from the *Guiron* prologue is that the production of French literature is a collective enterprise involving both knights and clerics, and that each individual romance, far from standing alone, is an integral part of the overall corpus.[30]

Just as the whole tradition of medieval French romance presents itself as an "overall corpus" that derives its individual parts from translations of a mythical Ur-text written in Latin, I argued that the whole of Ferdowsi's *Shāhnāma* derives itself from a comparable Ur-text written in Pahlavi.[31]

Following my analysis of the "mystical gift" and the "regenerated {50} archetype" passages in the *Shāhnāma*, Nagy interprets them as evidence for the kind of culture "where written text and oral tradition coexist."[32] In such cultures, as Nagy argues, "the idea of a written text can even become a primary metaphor for the authority of recomposition-in-performance."[33] The consequences are enormous:

> The intrinsic applicability of *text* as metaphor for *recomposition-in-performance* helps explain a type of myth, attested in a wide variety of cultural contexts, where the evolution of a poetic tradition, moving slowly ahead in time until it reaches a relatively static phase, is

28. Lathuillère 1966:176, translated by Huot 1991:218.
29. Lathuillère 1966:177.
30. Huot 1991:218.
31. Davidson 2013a[1994]:35–39.
32. Nagy 1996a:70.
33. Nagy 1996a:70.

> reinterpreted by the myth as if it resulted from a single incident, pictured as the instantaneous recovery or even regeneration of a lost text, an archetype. In other words, myth can make its own "big bang" theory for the origins of epic, and it can even feature in its scenario the concept of writing.[34]

In brief, the Persian model of a "regenerated archetype" of the *Shāhnāma* reveals "a myth about the synthesis of oral traditions that is articulated in terms of written traditions."[35]

For Nagy, the most striking comparative parallel with the Persian model is a set of ancient Greek myths that tell of the disintegration and subsequent reintegration of the Homeric corpus itself, culminating in the historicized narrative of the "Peisistratean Recension."[36] Other comparable parallels include the medieval Irish {51} aetiology of the "lost" book of the *Cattle Raid of Cúailgne*.[37] Another parallel adduced by Nagy is the medieval French narrative of *Guiron le courtois*, as quoted above, which "lays the foundation for its authority by telling of the many French books that were produced from what is pictured as an archetypal translation of a mythical Latin book of the Holy Grail."[38] Yet another parallel comes from ethnographic fieldwork on the oral epic tradition of an illiterate society, the untouchable Malas of India: "The epic, it is claimed [by the performers], was first written by a Brahmin poet, torn into shreds, discarded, and then picked up by the present performers."[39]

We can supplement the parallel that I adduced in my first book for the *Shāhnāma*, from the French *Guiron le courtois*, with two more parallels adduced by Davis in a 1996 article, one from the *Historia Regum Britanniae* of

34. Nagy 1996a:70.

35. Nagy 1996a:70.

36. Nagy 1996a:71–72, with bibliography. Omidsalar 2011:162–163 voices his opinion that Nagy's "absentminded" account of Ferdowsi's narrative about the *Shāhnāma*'s disintegration and reintegration in his foreword to the first edition of Davidson 2013a[1994] (p. ix) has been fabricated by means of an illusory comparison with the narrative of the Peisitratean recension of Homer, which Nagy "imposes" on Ferdowsi. Despite Omidsalar's protestations, Nagy's interpretation of Ferdowsi's aetiological narrative remains for me both valid and insightful. I would also like to take this opportunity to object to the subtitle of the concluding chapter of Omidsalar 2011 ("*Shāhnāmeh* and the Tyranny of Eurocentrism") and to the subsequent offensive language of that same chapter, where Nagy serves as the initial (perhaps archetypal) victim of Omidsalar's denigration of the "callousness and arrogance" shown by Western academics in their approach to the *Shāhnāma*.

37. Nagy 1996a:70, following J. F. Nagy 1985:292–293.

38. Nagy 1996a.71; cf. Davidson 2013a[1994]:38n43.

39. Blackburn 1989:32n25; cf. Nagy 1996a:71.

Geoffrey of Monmouth and the other from the *Brut* of Layamon.[40] In the case of Geoffrey (ca. 1150 CE), his prologue about "a very ancient book" (*vetustissimus liber*) that had once been given to him by a "friend" (one "Walter of Oxford") is comparable to the ancient book given to Ferdowsi by his mysterious "friend." There are further analogies to be drawn from Layamon's *Brut*:

> The picture of an author gathering together his sources, collating them and beginning work, is in essence very similar to the one given at the beginning of the *Shāhnāmeh*, where Ferdowsī speaks of a dehqan's gathering (*farāham āvordan*) of scattered texts which were then reduced to one narrative, and {52} both Ferdowsī and Layamon insist on the added authority of unfamiliar or ancient languages.[41]

With reference to the Persian theme of a *dehqān*'s "gathering (*farāham āvordan*) of scattered texts which were then reduced to one narrative," we may compare again the Greek myths that tell of the disintegration and subsequent reintegration of the Homeric corpus, culminating in historicized narratives about the "Peisistratean Recension."[42]

The historicized narratives about the so-called "Peisistratean Recension" lead to another important point of comparison. In the classical Persian traditions, as I have argued extensively in my earlier work, there is a comparable historicized narrative about a prose *Shāhnāma*, as reported in the so-called "older preface" to Ferdowsi's poetic *Shāhnāma*.[43] According to the "older preface," this prose *Shāhnāma* was commissioned by the "Lord of Ṭōs," Abu Manṣur ʿAbd al-Razzāq, and compiled by his secretary, Abu Manṣur Maʿmari (the project was reportedly completed in 346/April, 957 CE). Here is a key portion of the narrative:

> Therefore he [Abu Manṣur ʿAbd al-Razzāq] commanded his minister [*dastur*] Abu Manṣur Maʿmari to gather owners of books from among the *dehqān*-s, sages, and men of experience from various towns, and by his orders his servant (the said) Abu Manṣur Maʿmari compiled the book: he sent a person to various towns of Khorasan and brought wise men therefrom {53} [variant: and from elsewhere?], such as Mākh, son of Khorāsān, from Herāt; Yazdāndād, son of Shāpur, from Sistān; Māhōy Khorshēd, son of Bahrām, from Bishāpur; Shādān,

40. Davis 1996:48–51.
41. Davis 1996:50.
42. Nagy 1996a:93–112.
43. Davidson 1985:117, 123–126; 2013a[1994]:36–46.

> son of Borzin, from Ṭōs. He brought all four and set them down to produce those books of the kings, with their actions, their life-stories, the epochs of justice or injustice, troubles, wars, and the (royal) institutions, beginning with the first king [*key*] who was he who established the practices of civilization in the world and brought men out of (the condition of) beasts—down to Yazdgerd Shahriyār, who was the last of the Iranian kings.[44]

This narrative from the "older preface" has led to the common assumption that the book in question must have been Ferdowsi's own source.[45] In arguing against this assumption, I have pointed out that this historicized narrative is strikingly parallel to Ferdowsi's poetic narrative, as quoted above, concerning the genesis of the Book of Kings. We can also find other parallels in other preface narratives stemming from other branches of the *Shāhnāma* textual tradition.[46] In one such parallel narrative, it is King Anōshirvān (reign: 531–579 CE) who commissioned a collection, from all the {54} provinces in his empire, of popular stories concerning ancient kings.[47] In another such narrative, the last Sasanian king, Yazdgerd (reign: 632–651 CE), commissions the *dehqān* Dāneshvar to reassemble the Book of Kings.[48] On the basis of such parallel versions, I argued that the version of the "older preface," even if it has a historical basis, "conforms nevertheless to a mythmaking pattern that keeps revalidating the Book of Kings by way of explaining its 'origins'."[49] In other words, the version of the "older preface" counts as a variant in its own right:

> The greater density of historical information in the "prose preface" version need not take it out of consideration as a variant. Cross-cultural studies of interaction between the myths and historical events that are independently known to have taken place show

44. Translation by Minorsky 1964:266. For a defense of the reading "Bishāpur," see Shahbazi 1991:36n96.

45. Already Nöldeke 1930; cf. Shahbazi 1991:37, with qualifications. Further qualifications in Blois 2004[1992–1997]:1.108–110, who finds numerous "contradictions" between Ferdowsi's *Shāhnāma* and what he reconstructs for the prose *Shāhnāma*. Blois concludes, p. 110: "It would seem much more likely that Firdausi had the (then relatively new) *Shāh-nāmah* of Abū Manṣūr at his disposal only at the time when he was writing the final section of his poem (that devoted to the Sasanians) and that for the earlier sections (the bulk of the work) he depended on one of the earlier Persian translations of the Book of Kings. In short, though there can be no doubt that Firdausi's poem is based on written sources, we cannot necessarily presume that it is at all based on a single source."

46. See Davidson 2013a[1994]:44, with references.

47. Davidson 2013a[1994]:44.

48. Davidson 2013a[1994]:44.

49. Davidson 2013a[1994]:44–45.

> that myths tend to appropriate and then reorganize historical information. As for Ferdowsi's own version of the story, it is more versatile because it is more stylized and therefore generic. Ferdowsi's version of how the Book of Kings came about can usurp more specific versions because it is so generic. His version implicitly acknowledges the variation of these stories by avoiding specificity in referring to the persons, places, or time involved in the genesis of his own source "book" for the *Shāhnāma*. And by acknowledging this multiformity, Ferdowsi is in effect transcending it. His *Shāhnāma* does not depend on any one version for the establishment of a text. The myth gives validity to the text by making the assembly of wise and pious men in the community the collective source of the text.[50]

{55} My argument that the narrative of the "prose preface" is driven by mythological themes necessitated by the prestige of the very idea of a Book of Kings has recently been supported by Davis, who has developed further arguments against the simplistic notion that it was merely the historical details about Abu Manṣur ʿAbd al-Razzāq that drove the narrative of the prose preface.[51]

For another example of mythological themes that drive narratives explaining the genesis of books, I cite the prooemium of the *Zartoshtnāma* (ca. 978 CE), where the poet claims that he has turned an ancient book, written in Pahlavi, into Persian poetry.[52] Yet another example is the narrative tradition about the Persian version of *Kalīla and Dimna*:

> A similar argument can be made concerning a Pahlavi version, produced in the reign of Khosrow I Anōshirvān (531–579 CE), of the Indic corpus of fables known as the *Pañcatantra*; the Arabic version of Ibn al-Muqaffaʿ, apparently based on the Pahlavi version, is known by the title *Kalīla and Dimna* ... There was a version of *Kalīla and Dimna* in Persian, composed in verse by the poet Rōdaki and commissioned by Abuʾl-Fażl Balʿāmi, vizier to the Samanid king Naṣr II Ibn Aḥmad [reign: 914–943 CE]; this poem is not extant, except for some fragments. Ferdowsi himself draws a parallel between his own *Shāhnāma* and Rōdaki's *Kalīla and Dimna*, stressing that the uniqueness of both compositions depends on what is described as the turning of prose into poetry (*Shāhnāma* VIII 655.3460–3464).[53]

50. Davidson 2013a[1994]:45.

51. Davis 1996. These arguments are useful in countering the approach of Alishan 1989 to myths in epic, as analyzed in Essay Six.

52. Details in Davidson 2013a[1994]:36–37.

53. Davidson 2013a[1994]:38.

{56} Here I disagree with Blois, who takes literally all such references to the turning of Pahlavi prose into Persian poetry.[54] Also, he thinks that such poetry is merely "versification":

> The Arabic text [of the *Kalīla and Dimna*] has a number of times been translated back into (Neo-)Persian. The oldest translation, sponsored by the well known Samanid wazīr Balʿāmī and mentioned in Firdawsī's *Shāhnāma*, . . . is lost. That version was apparently the basis for the Persian versification by the celebrated poet Rōdakī, of which scattered verses have survived.[55]

Because Blois assumes that oral traditions exclude written traditions, for him the poetry of Rōdakī is in this case merely the "versification" of prosaic content. He makes a parallel assumption about the poetry of Ferdowsi as merely a "versification" of Persian prose translations of an earlier Pahlavi prose account, the *Khwadāynāmag*.[56] I have argued against such an assumption in the case of the *Shāhnāma*,[57] and also in the case of the *Kalīla and Dimna*:

> Here again it is unjustified to posit a Persian prose archetype for the Persian poetry of the *Kalīla and Dimna* merely on the basis of references to an authoritative book of prose as source. The implicit equation of "prose" with Pahlavi documents conveys an authority that is comparable to the medium of Ferdowsi's poetry. In this medium, as we have seen, {57} both the Pahlavi book *and* oral poetic traditions are visualized as the basis for a poem's authority.[58]

As we have seen, the *Shāhnāma* contains one of the "versified" versions of the story of the origins of the *Kalīla and Dimna*—versions that go beyond the content of what Blois supposes to be the prosaic source. According to Blois, the role played by Borzōy in his quest for the *Kalīla and Dimna* "has been inflated to absurd proportions" by the *Shāhnāma* and other retellings.[59]

Such is the fate of Ferdowsi's poetic craft at the hands of Blois. Written sources are being "versified" and thereby "inflated." Since Blois thinks that oral poetic traditions cannot tap into lore that derives from written sources, as in the case of the *Kalīla and Dimna*, he cannot conceive of the

54. Blois 1990:5, 51–57. His difficulties in explaining all the narratives in terms of textual stemmata become especially evident at p. 57.

55. Blois 1990:5; emphasis mine.

56. Blois 1990:51–57, esp. p. 51.

57. Davidson 2013a[1994]:38–39.

58. Davidson 2013a[1994]:38.

59. Blois 1990:53.

elaboration of such lore by way of oral poetic traditions. For him, the esthetics of poetic elaboration become mere inflations of historical facts. For him, the *Shāhnāma* is a versified inflation of a prosaic exemplar. I prefer to view Ferdowsi's poetry as a re-creation, through living oral traditions, of lore learned from both books and "singers":

> Ferdowsi's claim, that he received an old Pahlavi Book of Kings, written in prose, and that he turned it into poetry—the first, the best, and therefore the only *Shāhnāma*—could not have been made without the authority of the oral poetic traditions that he had mastered. The idea of the book contains, like a time-capsule, not only an idealized composition-in-performance but also, cumulatively, an idealized sum total of all oral poetic traditions as they were performed before Ferdowsi and as they {58} continued to be performed after Ferdowsi. As such, the book is both a concrete object and a symbol, expressing the authority and authenticity of the oral poetic traditions that are being performed.[60]

60. Davidson 2013a[1994]:46.

Essay Four

An Opposing View

"Merely Retelling What They Found in a 'Book'"

{59} In the first fascicule of *Persian Literature* 5, intended as a continuation of Charles Ambrose Storey's unfinished *Persian Literature: A Bio-Bibliographical Survey*,[1] François de Blois launches his enterprise with a first chapter bearing the ambitious title "The Origins of Persian Poetry."[2] After summarizing various received opinions about "early Persian narrative poems,"[3] Blois makes this sweeping claim about their authors:

> Despite the insistence by the authors of these narratives that they are merely [*sic*] retelling what they found in a 'book', attempts have occasionally been made to view early Persian poetry in the light of the well-known theory of 'oral poetry,' a theory which has had a very strong influence particularly on the Anglo-Saxon school of Homeric studies, but [*sic*] which has also been applied with interesting results to such fields as pre-Islamic Arabic poetry.[4]

The placement of "but" here reveals a negative attitude on the part of Blois, but it is not clear whether his negativity has to do with "the well-known theory of 'oral poetry'" or with "the Anglo-Saxon school of Homeric studies" or with both. Other things too are left unclear. For example, Blois never says what exactly he {60} means by "the Anglo-Saxon school of Homeric studies." Nor does he name those who have produced "interesting results" in applying oral poetics to such fields as pre-Islamic Arabic poetry.[5] Nor does he indicate why and how these results are "interesting" to him. The reader finds no footnotes here about any of these questions. There is in fact only one footnote that anchors any of his claims in the context of the blanket assertion as I have quoted it immediately above, and that is a single reference, at the point where he speaks of "the well-known theory of 'oral

1. Storey 1927–.
2. Blois 2004[1992–1997]:1.44–57.
3. Blois 2004[1992–1997]:1.52.
4. Blois 2004[1992–1997]:1.53.
5. I can think of two main possibilities: Monroe 1972 and Zwettler 1978.

poetry'," to an article I published in 1984.[6] In his footnote, he refers to no other bibliography besides that article.

After this sweeping statement, just as I have quoted it, we find a mere four pages[7] in support of the claim that the authors of early Persian narrative "are merely [*sic*] retelling what they found in a 'book'."[8] Blois starts by attempting to anticipate an objection, with reference to passages in the *Shāhnāma* where the poet Ferdowsi "states, or implies, that he has heard the story he is about to tell from an 'old *dihqān*' or the like."[9] At this point he appends a footnote referring to "the collection of passages" in my 1985 article.[10] (I have since reworked this collection in my first book.)[11] As in his immediately preceding footnote, about "the well-known theory of 'oral poetry'," Blois refers to no other bibliography besides my {61} article. After this second reference to my work, I am never heard of again as Blois proceeds to claim that "it is much more likely that in all the passages of this sort the poet is merely repeating, in verse, the statement by his written source that it has derived its information [*sic*] from the person in question."[12]

This claim of Blois, as we will see, is not original. As for the main argument that he produces to back up his claim,[13] it is not original either, as we will also see presently; in fact, his argumentation depends on assumptions against which I have already formulated counter-arguments in my 1985 article.[14] These counter-arguments are simply ignored by Blois.

Before we assess the value of the argumentation offered by Blois in *Persian Literature* 5, I take note of his retrospective opinion in Blois 1998, published six years later, in his review of my first book:

> [A]lready in 1992, in the continuation [*sic*] of Storey's *Persian literature*, V/1, pp. 42–58, I have discussed and rebutted the principal arguments in part II [of Davidson 1985] (now part I [of Davidson 2013a[1994]]) of Davidson's paper, namely her contention that Firdawsi's *Shāhnāma* is not primarily dependent on written sources, but should be analysed

6. Davidson 1985.
7. Blois 2004[1992–1997]:1.53–56.
8. Blois 2004[1992–1997]:1.53. This view of Blois is supported by Meisami 1993:262.
9. Blois 2004[1992–1997]:1.53.
10. Davidson 1985:113–115.
11. Davidson 2013a[1994]:30–33. The second edition of Blois 2004[1992–1997] notes as much (p. 56), although the author characterizes my expanded treatment as a merely "slight reworking."
12. Blois 2004[1992–1997]:1.53. I have already referred to the qualifications added by Blois 2004[1992–1997]:1.108–110, where he concedes that Ferdowsi's *Shāhnāma* depends on not just *one* written source, i.e. not just on the Abū Manṣūr ʿAbd al-Razzāq text.
13. Blois 2004[1992–1997]:1.53–56.
14. Davidson 1985, reworked in Davidson 2013a[1994]:33–46.

> as "oral poetry." Since the author has not in any way improved on her previous arguments, nor has she responded to the criticism which has been brought against them, and since this reviewer does not share the author's fondness for {62} regurgitating earlier publications, I shall, perhaps, be excused from the duty of commenting yet again on the first part of the book under review.[15]

Looking back at the words of Blois in his earlier piece, I see no successful rebuttal of my principal arguments.[16] What I do see instead is a misunderstanding or even misrepresentation of these arguments, and an outright ignoring of the counter-arguments that I had already formulated in my 1985 article[17] in opposition to the assumptions of scholars whom Blois is following, most notably Nöldeke.[18] Like Nöldeke, Blois insists that poets like Ferdowsi were "merely retelling what they found in a 'book'."[19]

My main thesis in Davidson 1985 had been formulated not negatively, "that the *Shāhnāma* is not primarily dependent on written sources," but positively: that it *can* be analyzed as "oral poetry." Furthermore, my 1985 article had made it clear that "oral poetry" in medieval Persian traditions is not at all incompatible with "written sources," and my first book makes this point even clearer, improving on my argumentation by adducing further comparative and internal evidence.[20] Another improvement in the 1994 version of my argumentation is the added feature of a detailed critique of the valuable work of Shahbazi.[21] In the context of my ongoing friendly {63} debate with Shahbazi, I have developed counter-arguments to his thesis that the sources of Ferdowsi, even in contexts where the poet says that he heard the performer perform, were exclusively texts.[22]

With reference to the approach of scholars who try to extrapolate a historical account of Ferdowsi's poetic career on the basis of (1) the prefaces to the *Shāhnāma* and (2) various passages taken from the *Shāhnāma* itself,[23] I offer an alternative approach:

15. Blois 1998:269.
16. Blois 2004[1992–1997]:1.44–57.
17. Davidson 1985:116–121.
18. Nöldeke 1930.
19. See also Meisami 1993:262, who agrees with Blois.
20. See especially Davidson 2013a[1994]:24–25, 26–27, 40–41.
21. Shahbazi 1991.
22. Davidson 2013a[1994]:27n14, 28n15, 41n57, 44n71, and especially 45n72. See also p. 25 on the implications of the references to the patronage of Maḥmud of Ghazna; p. 27 about questions of dictation; pp. 29, 37, 44 about stylized references to occasions of composition; p. 38 on parallelisms of source-claims for the *Shāhnāma* and the *Kalīla and Dimna*.
23. Shahbazi 1991:68–71.

> I stress that my goal is not to deny the likelihood that some of the declarations by the poet within the poem, especially concerning such details as his precise age at various stages of his composing the *Shāhnāma*, are based on historical fact (Shahbazi's book is particularly valuable in offering a rich collection of such details). Rather, I repeat my earlier argument that such details cannot be treated as raw data about the real life and times of the poet but as part of a traditional discourse that incorporates factual details into an ongoing reinterpretation of the poem's role in society. We may say that such reinterpretation operates on the principles of myth, provided we understand myth in the sense of a given society's codification of its own truth-values.[24]

Let us return once more to the claim of Blois that Ferdowsi and other authors of early Persian narrative "are merely [*sic*] retelling {64} what they found in a 'book.'"[25] His primary argument in support of this claim is that Ferdowsi refers to as many as three of the four figures who are identified by the "prose preface" as compilers of the "prose *Shāhnāma*."[26] In making his case, Blois is actually anticipated by Shahbazi,[27] whose arguments are countered already in my book.[28] In his review of my first book, Blois fails to give credit to Shahbazi for having anticipated his primary argument and, needless to say, he also fails to give me credit for the counter-argument in my book. In any case, as I have already noted, the case made by Blois is anticipated by Nöldeke.[29]

In his earlier work, Blois simply ignored my argumentation against a literal-minded interpretation of the "prose preface" of the "prose *Shāhnāma*."[30] Six years later, in reviewing my first book, he also ignored Davis' 1996 article, which likewise argues against such an interpretation, and which joins the stance of my first book in arguing for an oral poetic tradition as the foundation of Ferdowsi's *Shāhnāma*.[31] As I have already noted in Essays Two

24. Davidson 2013a[1994]:28n15, with reference to Nagy 1990b:436 on the uses of myth in contexts of authorial self-definition.

25. Blois 2004[1992–1997]:1.53.

26. Blois 2004[1992–1997]:1.53–56.

27. Shahbazi 1991:133–134n87.

28. Davidson 2013a[1994], esp. p. 45n72.

29. On the arguments of Nöldeke 1930:62, see again Davidson 2013a[1994]:34–35.

30. Blois 2004[1992–1997]:1.53–56, ignoring Davidson 1985:111–127.

31. Blois 1998, ignoring Davis 1996. See again Davis 1996 pp. 48n1 and 53n22, with reference to Davidson 2013a[1994]. Blois 1998 cannot be excused for having ignored Davis 1996 on the grounds that his review appeared two years later: as we saw earlier, Blois relies in his 1998 review on a publication as recent as Herrmann 1997. To his credit, Blois finally demonstrates an awareness of Davis' work and its relationship to my own work in the second edition of Blois

and Three, Davis agrees with my contention that there are traces of an oral tradition reflected in Ferdowsi's stylized references to his sources—not only where {65} Ferdowsi speaks of antecedent performances that he had heard but even where he refers to an archetypal Book of Kings.[32] Davis supports my thesis that Ferdowsi's stylized poetic references to an archetypal source-book reflect a "rhetoric" of oral poetics.[33]

Here is how I conclude my argumentation against the theory that the "prose *Shāhnāma*" of Abu Manṣur ʿAbd al-Razzāq was the source of Ferdowsi's poetic *Shāhnāma*:

> Of the three multiform stories [here I am not counting the *Shāhnāma* version] concerning the constitution or reconstitution of the Book of Kings, the one in the "older preface" is the least essential for the purposes of understanding the composition of the Ferdowsi's *Shāhnāma*. To motivate the constitution of a Persian prose *Shāhnāma* is to motivate something less prestigious, and from hindsight, less enduring. In the end this version can after all survive only as an intrusion in the text of the poetic *Shāhnāma*. Ferdowsi's *Shāhnāma* needs no prose introduction, because it introduces itself poetically. By contrast, it is a prosaic *Shāhnāma* that would really require a prosaic introduction. It seems to me ironic that this unattested prosaic *Shāhnāma*, of which we know only by way of its reconstructed prosaic preface, should be treated in current scholarship as the source of Ferdowsi's poetry.[34]

{66} Following my analysis of Ferdowsi's references to an archetypal source-book, Nagy interprets them as evidence for the kind of culture "where

---

2004[1992–1997] (p. 56). Ironically, however, Blois mentions my work and that of Davis more or less merely as an opportunity to criticize us both for having overlooked in the first edition of Davidson 2013a[1994] and in Davis 1996 respectively his pertinent remarks in the first fascicle of the first edition of Blois 2004[1992–1997]. The irony resides in the fact that Blois in 2004 fails to make any mention whatsoever of the first edition of the present book (2000), in which I responded at length to his 1992 (and 1998) criticism of my work. Blois is in the habit of denouncing others for their lack of familiarity with relevant scholarship, and yet in this instance he himself is several years behind the times.

32. See again Part 1 of Davidson 2013a[1994] (pp. 13–62), and my earlier discussion in Davidson 1985:105–142, where I also address the problem of the "prose preface" to the *Shāhnāma*. My arguments about the "prose preface" in Davidson 2013a[1994]:24–46 are supported by the arguments of Davis 1996.

33. Davis 1996:48–51. Thus the article of Davis helps refute the negative arguments of Blois 2004[1992–1997] against Davidson 1985 and of Blois 1998 against Davidson 2013a[1994].

34. Davidson 2013a[1994]:45–46. For further arguments against the privileging of the narrative to be found in the "prose preface" over other variant narratives, see Davis 1996.

written text and oral tradition coexist."[35] In positing such a coexistence, he is following the later work of Lord 1991 and 1995, who explored the interactions of oral and written traditions in a variety of cultures.[36] In light of Lord's work, it is a pity that critics like Blois persist in assuming that the very existence of written traditions disproves, of and by itself, the possibility of any coexistence with oral traditions.[37] In arguing against me, Blois makes it seem as if any proof of the use of written traditions is in itself a disproof of any use of oral traditions.[38] And yet, he disingenuously claims to have rebutted my "contention" that "Firdawsi's *Shāhnāma* is not *primarily* [*sic*] dependent on written sources, but should be analysed as 'oral poetry'."[39] He makes it seem as if I, not he, were the one who assumes that oral poetry cannot coexist with written traditions. But that is exactly what he assumes.[40]

In pursuing his claim that Ferdowsi and other authors of early Persian narrative "are merely [*sic*] retelling what they found in a 'book'," Blois also argues that some of Ferdowsi's wordings "can only be explained in terms of the misreading of written sources."[41] He has in mind various spelling pronunciations, as they are called {67} by linguists. He offers as an example the form "Nastur," which seems to be a mispointing, by way of Arabic script, for Bastur (cf. Middle Persian *bstwl*, Avestan *Bastauuairī-*).[42] Blois is here overlooking something quite obvious: in any culture, "wrong" spelling pronunciations can leak into the everyday spoken language, where they are free to spread irreversibly. Once a form becomes part of the spoken language, it can become part of an oral tradition. It is wrong for Blois to claim, as he does in the name of "the adherents of the theory of oral poetry," that the "prerequisite of this theory is precisely the assumption of an uninterrupted oral tradition from antiquity to the present day."[43] What does he mean by "uninterrupted?" That there is no change in oral tradition? He has not even thought of the most obvious empirically observable fact about oral traditions: that they are fed by the everyday spoken language, and that they evolve along with the spoken language.[44]

35. Nagy 1996a:70.
36. The views of Lord in these later works have been assessed in Essay Two above.
37. Blois 2004[1992–1997]:1.53–56.
38. Blois 2004[1992–1997]:1.53–56.
39. Blois 1998:269.
40. Blois 2004[1992–1997]:1.53–56.
41. Blois 2004[1992–1997]:1.54.
42. Blois 2004[1992–1997]:1.55.
43. Blois 2004[1992–1997]:1.55.
44. I am surprised that Blois 2004[1992–1997]:1.54 assumes that Tūr in the *Shāhnāma* can be explained simply in terms of a "mispointing (again conceivable only in Arabic script) for

When Blois insists that poets like Ferdowsi were "merely [*sic*] retelling what they found in a 'book'," his wording reveals a curious attitude toward classical Persian poetry. For him, the poetics of Ferdowsi is reduced to a "retelling" of prose narrative in poetic narrative, and the reductiveness is made clear by the placement of "merely." According to this reductionistic scenario, Ferdowsi first reads something in prose and then he "merely" retells it in "versified" {68} form.[45] This is to misread and even slight the power of poetry—"oral" or otherwise. My understanding is different, as I made it clear in Essay Three: even in situations where the poetry of Ferdowsi may happen to draw from a written source, the actual process of "retelling" is still an art form of poetic re-creation. The same goes for situations where the poetry of Ferdowsi happens to draw from an oral traditional source. Either way, whether the immediate narrative source of Ferdowsi is "oral" or written, I hold that the actual process of his narration is a matter of oral poetics.

As I look back one last time at "The Origins of Persian Poetry," this first of chapters in what Blois calls his "continuation" of another man's work, I must in the end reject his reductionistic views of these "origins."[46] I prefer instead the vision of Gilbert Lazard, who argues that the development of Persian literature

> was neither a pure and simple resurgence of the ancient culture nor the expression of an entirely fresh culture of Arab-Islamic origin. The links with ancient Iran had been established partly perhaps by such of the Middle Persian writings as were still being read, but surely much more by what had been handed down to Arabic literature and what still remained, more or less modified and brought up to date, <u>in the living oral tradition</u>. It is in these two sources, Arabic literature and <u>oral Iranian literature</u>, that the origin of the forms and themes of Persian poetry must be sought.[47]

Tūz- [as in Thaᶜālibī], representing Middle-Persian *twc*." How does Blois explain the Avestan forms *tūra-* and *tūiriia-* 'Turanian', presupposing aetiologically the "ancestor" Tūr?

45. Blois 2004[1992–1997]:1.52: "versifications of pre-existing written narratives."

46. I also resist, as I noted earlier, the views of Blois concerning "a system of accentual metre" (2004[1992–1997]:1.44).

47. Lazard 1975:612; emphasis mine. Also quoted by Meisami 1987:10. Since Meisami is thanked by Blois 2004[1992–1997]:1.xiii (cf. p. 3 of the first edition) as one of those who agreed to read and comment on his prepublished manuscript, I find it all the more curious that he ignores the assessment of Lazard and others concerning the role of oral poetry in the evolution of Persian literature. On the term "oral literature" see Lord 1991:2–3, 16, with further comments by Nagy 1996a:13.

Essay Five

Rostam the Crown-Bestower

{71} This essay re-examines a comparison, developed in my earlier work, between the Persian hero Rostam as guardian of the *farr* or 'luminous glory' of the Keyānid *shāh*-s in the *Shāhnāma* of Ferdowsi on one hand and, on the other, the Avestan god Apąm Napāt as guardian of the *x*ᵛ*arənah*—a prototype of Persian *farr*—as the 'luminous glory' of solar power in *Yašt* 19 of the *Avesta*.[1] Central to this re-examination is the poetic epithet of Rostam, *tājbakhsh* 'crown-bestower', as deployed by Ferdowsi in the *Shāhnāma*. I will argue that the meaning of this epithet, if not the actual idea of a crown, can be traced back to an Indo-Iranian tradition, and ultimately to an Indo-European tradition, just as the Avestan name Apąm Napāt goes back to an Indo-Iranian tradition, and ultimately to an Indo-European tradition. Decisive pieces of comparative evidence, I hope to show, come from (1) the vast body of documentation concerning an ancient Indic royal consecration ritual known as the *rājasūya*, (2) a key passage in Book 2 of the *Mahābhārata*, and (3) the narrative of Theseus' submarine encounter with both his would-be mother, the Nereid Amphitrite, and her likewise Nereid entourage, in Ode 17 of Bacchylides.[2]

Before we consider the semantics of the Persian epithet *tājbakhsh* 'crown-bestower,' it is important to review the traditions associated with the Avestan god Apąm Napāt. The divine name Apąm Napāt has a cognate in the Indic Vedas: Vedic Apām Napāt is likewise a {72} god, as celebrated in *Rig Veda* 2.35. The Avestan-Vedic parallelisms in form and theme have led to the reconstruction of the Indo-Iranian figure Apām Napāt.[3] Clearly, Apām Napāt

1. Davidson 1985:67–103 and ch. 5 of Davidson 2013a[1994] (pp. 85–97). For an overview of the influence of Iranian oral traditions on the *Shāhnāma* of Ferdowsi, see Skjærvø 1994:205–207, 240 and Skjærvø 1998b. For the derivation of Avestan *x*ᵛ*arənah* from *x*ᵛ*ar-* 'sun', and for an overall discussion of Iranian myths about gods and heroes connected with the concept of *x*ᵛ*arənah* as solar power, see Puhvel 1987:277–283. For more on *Yašt* 19, see Skjærvø 1994:217–219 and 1996b:602, 613. On the oral traditional background of the Avestan hymns see Skjærvø 1994, esp. p. 200. For an assessment of some of the relevant trends in Avestan scholarship, see Skjærvø 1996a . On some of the relatively recent innovations in Avestan scholarship, see Skjærvø 1997b.

2. I owe this insight to John McDonald.

3. Dumézil 1968–1973:3.21–89; Nagy 1980:170–172, 1990a:100–102 (these pages contain a a revised version of Nagy 1980); Puhvel 1987:277–283.

is a god in both the Avestan and the Vedic traditions,[4] but the actual words *Apām Napāt* mean much more than just the name of a god: Apām Napāt is the 'descendent of the waters', which is a *kenning* that expresses the mystical idea of fire-in-water.[5] In Indic traditions, the mystical referent of the kenning is the fire-god Agni, who is reborn every morning as the solar fire that rises out of the depths of the earth-encircling cosmic waters; as we see from *Rig Veda* 2.35, this macrocosmic fire of the sun corresponds to the microcosmic fire of sacrifice, and both fires come together in the figure of the Indic god of sacrifice, Agni.[6]

The kenning of "fire-in-water" is not only Indo-Iranian: it is even older, of Indo-European provenience.[7] We can find thematic cognates of Indo-Iranian Apām Napāt in other Indo-European {73} languages, as in the case of the Old Norse skaldic kenning *sævar niðr* 'kinsman of the sea', referring to fire.[8] Such a kenning tells a micro-narrative, which is actually contained in the epithet Apām Napāt.[9]

Moreover, this kenning about the progeny of the waters is a sacred myth, and its micro-narrative is contained in the names of the Roman god *Neptūnus*, as celebrated in the cult myth of the Feast of the Neptunalia on July 23, and of the Irish mythological figure *Nechtan*, custodian of a magic mound that hides a secret well radiating heat and light.[10]

In the Irish myth, the dangerous fire in the well makes the waters burst forth to become the river Boyne as it flows to the sea, from where it takes a submarine and then subterranean course, "reemerging to form many of the world's great rivers, only to return in the end to Nechtan's mound."[11]

4. Boyce 1975; also 1986:149: "What is indisputable with regard to the Iranian Apąm Napāt is that this name represents a powerful divinity, an Ahura, a close partner of Mithra, who, though still daily honoured through the Zoroastrian liturgies, has ceased to be popularly worshipped."

5. Watkins 1995:45, 153, 254. For an Armenian parallel to the Indo-Iranian kenning of Apām Napāt, see Watkins pp. 167, 254, who adduces the myth of the birth of Vahagn, preserved in Movsēs Xorenacʿi, *History of the Armenians* 1.31 (following the Armenian text as established by Russell 1987:196).

6. Nagy 1990a:100. As Watkins p.254n18 argues, "The gender-marked kinship term *nápāt* reflects the masculine *Agni*." By contrast, Boyce has a theory concerning an "identification of Iranian Apąm Napāt as Varuṇa" (1986:149, with reference to Boyce 1975), on which see further below.

7. For a summary, see Puhvel 1987:277–283, Chapter 16: "Fire in Water."

8. Puhvel 1987:278; cf. Watkins 1995:45, 153.

9. On epithets as containers of micro-narratives, see Nagy 1990a:22–23.

10. Summary and analysis of the Roman and Irish versions of the myth in Puhvel 1987:279–282. On names as containers of micro-narratives, see Nagy 1990b:207n35, with further references.

11. Puhvel 1987:279.

As for the corresponding Roman myth about the Alban Lake that threatens to flow into the sea, the historian Livy (5.16.9–11) "quotes" the words of the Delphic Oracle warning the Romans lest they "extinguish," paradoxically, the water of the lake, *aquam ... caue ... exstingues*: this formula, it can be argued, "slipped through the demythologizing fingers of Livy as a phraseological survival from the ritual of the Roman protomyth, a formula proper to the {74} *procuratio* of a theological prodigy, originally indicating what to do when there was eruptive fiery water pouring forth and running amok from Neptūnus' mythical lake."[12]

When it comes to Greece, we may compare the Hellenized place-name *Napas*, glossed in the dictionary of Hesychius as "an oil-producing well in the mountains of Persia," and the borrowed Greek word *náphtha* (cf. Indo-Iranian *naptya-*), which "we still use for the quintessential flammable liquid substance."[13] However, there also appears to be a native Greek verbal reflex of the Indo-European scion of the waters tradition in the rare word *népous*, which is used to describe the sea-god Proteus' seals at *Odyssey* 4.404, and which appears to derive from the same inherited lexeme **nepōt-* 'descendant' that yields the names of the aquatic divinities Apām Napāt, Nechtan and Neptūnus.[14] In fact this Homeric *hapax legomenon* occurs within the phrase νέποδες καλῆς ἁλοσύδνης, the last member of which is about as uncommon as its first, but which occurs elsewhere as an epithet of the sea-goddess Thetis, chief of the Nereids (*Iliad* 20.207), and of the Nereids in general (Apollonius *Argonautica* 4.1599). So in the syntactic unit νέποδες καλῆς ἁλοσύδνης "descendants of lovely Halosydne," that is, descendants of a marine goddess, we seem to be dealing with none other than a variation on the Indo-European formulaic expression 'descendant of the waters'. How appropriate, therefore, that the same passage of the *Odyssey* that refers to Proteus' seals as νέποδες also attributes to this same deity the ability to transform himself into καὶ ὕδωρ καὶ θεσπιαδὲς πῦρ "both water and magnificent fire" (4.418).[15]

In sum, although the Greek pantheon does not maintain the ancestral theonym that is the antecedent of the cognate appellations Apām Napāt, Nechtan, and Neptūnus, still a reflex of **nepōt-*, the form that inspires all of these names, is applied to the animals that are associated with Proteus, who is the functional congener of the Indo-Iranian, Irish and Roman figures in question, despite the fact that he is onomastically distinct from them.

12. Puhvel 1987:282.
13. Puhvel 1987:297, summarizing an earlier discussion in Puhvel 1973.
14. Louden 1999:73–74, endorsed by West 2007:271 and Oettinger 2009:190.
15. Louden 1999:74.

Furthermore, both another Greek sea-god, Poseidon, and his wife the Nereid Amphitrite are also involved in a mythological narrative that is apparently informed by the hereditary conceptual paradox of 'fire-in-water' similarly attached to Apām Napāt, Nechtan, Neptūnus, Proteus and the Nereid-epithet Halosydne.[16] The narrative in question is in fact that of Theseus' aforementioned encounter with Amphitrite and her companion Nereids, about which I made a passing remark in the opening paragraph of this essay, and to which I shall return below.[17]

The fullest argumentation about the Indo-European heritage of the sacred narrative of Apām Napāt is given by Georges Dumézil in the section of *Mythe et épopée* 3 entitled "La saison des rivières."[18] My own work on Apām Napāt has systematically applied the findings of Dumézil,[19] which in the meantime have been augmented by a wealth of supplementary findings.[20] I concentrated on the heroic rather than the divine aspects of the sacred narrative of the Indo-Iranian Apām Napāt, the essentials of which are more obvious from the Iranian, not the Indic, evidence. Puhvel offers the following summary:

> The Vedic god [Apām Napāt] has no obvious myth, but his characteristics, gleaned from the hymns, . . . mark him as a fiery deity immersed and inherent in watery depths, giving off light and lightning without visible energy source, and as a power that needs to be ritually placated for proper {75} utilization of waters. In this instance Iran contributes the story. *Yašt* 19 of the *Avesta*, celebrating the *x*^{v}*arənah* as the luminous and fiery hallmark of the duly elect king of Iran, tells of a mythical time when it became a pawn in the tug-of-war between the poles of Zoroastrian dualism (Spənta Mainyu and Angra Mainyu), in the course of which it withdrew from the fray in the direction of the mythical Lake Vourukaša. At that point Apām Napāt seized the *x*^{v}*arənah* and deposited it in the safety of the waters

16. See Louden 1999, whose analysis is anticipated to a certain extent by Gershenson 1991:87–88. For a recent endorsement of Louden's comparison see West 2007:270–2. Both Louden and West are apparently unaware of Gershenson's brief but similar and anterior remarks.

17. I am indebted to John McDonald for originally drawing my attention to the Greek comparanda—and to the work of Louden 1999. Also, I am most grateful to J.M. for helping me formulate the application of these Greek comparanda to the other comparative evidence that I have adduced.

18. Dumézil 1968–1973:3.19–89.

19. Davidson 1985:80–103, 2013a[1994]:98–113.

20. Especially Puhvel 1973, Ford 1974, Puhvel 1987:106, 120–121, 277–283, and Nagy 1990a:99–102, 118 (these pages contain a revised version of Nagy 1980).

> of the lake. Ahura-mazda thereupon declared open season on the *x^{v}arənah* as a legitimate goal of striving for qualified humans, holding out sacerdotal, pastoral, and martial rewards.[21]

I emphasize the idea of the *x^{v}arənah* "as a legitimate goal of striving," and that those who "strive" are "qualified humans." As we are told by *Yašt* 19, the first human who tried to seize *x^{v}arənah* was the Turanian Fraŋrasiian, who is the prototype of Afrāsiyāb, King of the Turanians and arch-enemy of the hero Rostam in the *Shāhnāma*. In the *Avesta*, there is no mention of Rostam, though the heroic themes associated with Rostam are implicit.[22] Instead of any direct heroic intervention, what we see in *Yašt* 19 is that the *x^{v}arənah* recoils by itself from the grasp of Fraŋrasiian the king, creating an outflow from the lake that leads into a multitude of rivers, one of which, the Haētumant, still contains the "escaped" *x^{v}arənah*: this river, the modern Helmand, "empties into the mythical lake, which is thus the beginning and end of earthly watercourses."[23]

Even though the hero Rostam is missing in the extant *Avesta*, {76} his arch-enemy Afrāsiyāb, so prominently featured in the *Shāhnāma*, is very much present in *Yašt* 19. To that extent, the heroic dimension of the sacred narrative is also present in *Yašt* 19, since the Turanian Afrāsiyāb is featured clearly on a human level. Moreover, the rescue of the *x^{v}arənah* by Apąm Napāt is also heroic *as an action*, even if the figure of Apąm Napāt is himself a god. Finally, the antagonism of Apąm Napāt toward Fraŋrasiian as a Turanian reveals that his deed of protecting the *x^{v}arənah* is a pro-Iranian action, parallel to the actions of Rostam in protecting the corresponding *farr* of the *shāh*-s. Here, then, is the essence of my drawing a parallel between the Avestan god Apąm Napāt and the Persian hero Rostam: as protectors of the *x^{v}arənah/farr* respectively, they are parallel in the action of a basic sacred narrative.[24]

This is not the same thing, however, as to claim that Apąm Napāt is Rostam, and I never make any such claim in my work. The actors in a sacred narrative may be gods or heroes. For example, in Indo-European myths about dragon-slaying, as encoded in such sacred micro-narratives as the Indic formula "Indra slew Vr̥tra" (*índro vr̥trám jaghāna* or *ahan*),[25] the sub-

21. Puhvel 1987:278–279.

22. See Skjærvø 1998b:162–164, who also analyses the aquatic metaphors inherent in the etymology of the Pahlavi form of Rostam's name, *Rōdstahm*.

23. Puhvel p. 279; cf. Davidson 2013a[1994]:103–104.

24. See especially Davidson 2013a[1994]:111–112. Cf. also Dumézil 1968–1973:2.180, 218–290 on narratives envisioning *x^{v}arənah* as a fiery essence lodged within a reed, parallel to the theme of a hero lodged within a reed.

25. Watkins 1995:301.

ject—the dragon-slayer—"is indifferently god (Zeus, Apollo, Thor, Indra) or man (Perseus, Kadmos, Herakles, Trita)."[26]

{77} It is therefore simply wrong of Blois (1998) to claim that I "identify" the god Apąm Napāt with the hero Rostam. With reference to my "name dropping" of Dumézil in Davidson 1994, here is what he says about my argumentation: "the upshot of her presentation is that she identifies Rustam with the Avestan deity Apąm Napāt (Vedic Apām Napāt), 'grandson [*sic*] of the waters'."[27] Blois goes on to say: "The identification is quite gratuitous."[28]

Blois explains his reasoning this way: "Apąm Napāt is not a warrior hero, but a god, an *ahura-* (like Ahura Mazdā and Miθra, and he is addressed, in the Avesta, as in the Veda, as the creator of mankind."[29] Such thinking shows no awareness of the extensive investigations concerning the systematic parallelisms of god and hero in Indo-Iranian sacred narrative. The most eminent example is Dumézil's *Mythe et épopée* 1 (1968), which explores the thematic and formal parallelisms linking gods and heroes in the *Mahābhārata*, especially in the case of the gods (1) Dharma (2) Indra plus Vāyu and (3) the twin Aśvins, corresponding to the heroes (1) Yudhiṣṭhira (2) Arjuna plus Bhīma, and (3) the twins heroes Nakula and Sahadeva.[30]

When Blois speaks in terms of an "identification" between one mythical figure and another, whether these figures be divine and {78} human, he is lapsing into an assumption that he is somehow dealing with historical figures. In my work, I explicitly reject this kind of a "prosopographical" approach to myth, arguing that the shaping of identities in mythical discourse is variable, depending on genre and context.[31] The wording of Blois in this matter is closely parallel to that of Alishan: "Ultimately Davidson's hypotheses [*sic*] argues for an identification of Rostam with the divinity Apām Napāt."[32]

In the case of Blois, there may be other reasons for his insistence on speaking in terms of an "identification" between Apąm Napāt and Rostam.

26. Watkins 1995:298. See especially his ch. 49: "From God to Hero: the Formulaic Network in Greek," pp. 471–482. See also his pp. 167, 254, comparing the Armenian traditions about Vahagn with the Indo-Iranian traditions about Apām Napāt. Cf. Puhvel 1987:121–122 on Rostam and his lineage: "the Sistanian dynasty is also [like the Keyānids] of patently mythical origin;" see also p. 242. On the Keyānids, see Dumézil 1986–1973:2.142–145.

27. Blois 1998:270; emphasis mine. On the semantics of Indo-European **nepōt-* see Puhvel 1987:277–278; cf. Dumézil 1968–1973:3.21n1 and Watkins 1995:254n18. In the case of Indo-Iranian **napāt-*, "proximity, intimacy, kinship are implied, not necessarily filiation" (Puhvel p. 278).

28. Blois 1998:270; again, emphasis mine.

29. Blois 1998:270.

30. See Skjærvø 1998b.

31. Davidson 2013a[1994]:105n25.

32. Alishan 1989:6; emphasis mine.

Here we may consider the usage of Mary Boyce, in an article that she published on Apąm Napāt in *Encyclopaedia Iranica*.[33] This article is cited by Blois as a key to refuting the "identification" that I supposedly made.[34]

For Boyce, the "identification" of Apąm Napāt is all-important. In her encyclopedia article, she relies on an earlier work of hers[35] in which she had argued that Apām Napāt is "an Indo-Iranian title" of the Vedic god Varuṇa, "whose apparent absence from the Iranian pantheon has always been a source of perplexity." Although she admits that "the identification of Iranian Apąm Napāt as Varuṇa remains controversial," nevertheless "a reasoned refutation of the hypothesis has yet to be published."[36]

Pursuing this "identification," Boyce insists that Apām Napāt as {79} "son of the waters" is a "water deity." She notes the application of the "title" Apām Napāt to the fire-god Agni and to the sun-god Savitr̥, explaining that "the original Apām Napāt had been an independent divinity, an Indo-Iranian 'water-spirit,' who had become associated with and partly absorbed in Agni because to ancient Indian thinkers water held fire within itself;"[37] also, "the link of this 'water-spirit' with Savitr̥ could be similarly explained because the setting sun was thought to sink into the seas beneath the earth."[38] Boyce seems to regard the theme of fire-in-water as merely an Indic mythical elaboration, adding: "in Indic rituals, as in Iranian ones, Apām Napāt's connection remained solely with water."[39]

While I agree with Boyce that Varuṇa as god of the earth-encircling waters overlaps in part with Apām Napāt, I disagree with her view that the theme of fire-in-water is merely an Indic mythical elaboration on the theme of the "Son of the Waters." This inherent theme of *Apām Napāt*, as we have seen, is not only Indo-Iranian but also Indo-European, centering on the sacred narrative of "fire-in-water." The fullest argumentation, as we have also seen, is given by Georges Dumézil in the section of *Mythe et épopée* 3 entitled "La saison des rivières."[40] In her *Encyclopaedia Iranica* article on Apąm Napāt, Boyce ignores Dumézil completely. She also ignores completely the related work of Jacques Duchesne-{80}Guillemin on the Iranian x^{v}*arənah*, which is essential to Dumézil's argumentation.[41]

My own work on Apąm Napāt has systematically applied the findings of

33. Boyce 1986.
34. Blois 1998:270. Alishan 1989:7 likewise sends me to Boyce 1986.
35. Boyce 1975.
36. Boyce 1986:149; emphasis mine.
37. Boyce 1986:149, following Oldenberg 1917:100–101, 113–114, 117–119.
38. Boyce 1986:149.
39. Boyce 1986:149; emphasis mine.
40. Dumézil 1968–1973:3.19–89.
41. Dumézil 1968–1973:24–27. See Duchesne-Guillemin 1963.

Dumézil.[42] When Blois dismisses my argumentation about Apąm Napāt by citing Boyce as a "good synthesis," he is relying on a work that fails to provide any counter-arguments to the findings of Dumézil. I find it ironic that Blois accuses me of "replacing rational argumentation by name dropping" when I apply the work of scholars like Dumézil.[43]

The basic problem with the work of Boyce on Apąm Napāt is that she does not appreciate the sacred narrative that is built into this name, because she has already "identified" Apąm Napāt as a god of waters. This sacred narrative, as Dumézil shows, concerns the sun as "fire-in-water," visualized in Iranian traditions as Avestan *x^varənah* and Persian *farr*.[44]

The Avestan version of Apām Napāt features a heroic deed connected with *xᵛarənah*. Any parallelism with Rostam is to be sought with reference to his own heroic deeds as connected with *farr*. In the *Shāhnāma*, this connection is thematically conveyed by way of the epithet *tājbakhsh* 'crown-bestower', which I have studied extensively in my earlier work.

{81} Another study of this epithet is that of Alishan.[45] Basically, Alishan follows Bivar, who argues that the "epic personality" of Rostam "represents an expansion of the hero of Carrhae," that is, the victorious Parthian general of the Surena clan who defeated the Roman army of Crassus at the Battle of Carrhae in 53 BCE, according to the narrative provided by Plutarch, *Life of Crassus* 21.6.[46] Alishan summarizes Bivar's argument this way:

> Bivar's evidence for this identification [*sic:* I note with interest the wording] is that both Rostam and the Surena are heroes from Sistān, both are connected to the Sakas, and whereas Rostam is distinguished in the *Shāhnāma* by the epithet *tājbakhsh* 'bestower of the crown', Surena also "held the privilege, hereditary in his family, of placing the diadem on the new sovereign's head at the coronation."[47]

Alishan tries to show how his explanation of the epithet is different from the one offered by Bivar, whose approach he describes as "the historical method."[48] When it comes to results, I cannot see any major difference, since the thesis of Alishan's argumentation is basically the same: that the

42. Davidson 1985:80–103, 2013a[1994]:98–113.

43. I may be faulted for not citing Boyce 1986 in Davidson 2013a[1994], but at least the works that I did cite provide support for my argumentation. The work cited by Blois 1998, by contrast, provides no support for his negative claims, since Boyce 1986 fails to provide any argumentation that addresses the findings of Dumézil about Apām Napāt.

44. For a summary, see again Puhvel 1987:106, 277–278, 281.

45. Alishan 1989.

46. Bivar 1980–1981:150.

47. Alishan 1989:5, quoting Bivar 1980–1981:144.

48. Alishan 1989:3.

epithet *tājbakhsh* derives ultimately from the historical event of the Parthian victory over the Roman army of Crassus at the Battle of Carrhae in 53 BCE.

Alishan also contrasts his approach with mine, which he calls "the socio-mythical method," and with that of Sarkārāti,[49] dubbed as "the legendary or epical method," in that Sarkārāti "argues that Rostam should be sought in neither history nor mythology but in {82} the legendary or epic tradition of the Saka people."[50] Sarkārāti is described as rejecting explanations "seeking one distinct historical personage for identifying Rostam."[51]

In describing my approach, Alishan begins by allowing that "Davidson avoids the fallacies of the historical method," and then he goes on to claim: "by misreading *tāj-bakhsh* as someone who has the power to 'confer' the '*farr* of the Keyānids ... upon them, she argues for the 'intrinsic' relationship of Rostam to the national epic tradition."[52] My reading of *tājbakhsh* is a "mis-reading" for Alishan because it takes the theme of a warrior's conferring sovereignty on a king well beyond the historical event of the Battle of Carrhae. Alishan, it seems, wants to derive the entire thematic legacy of the epithet *tājbakhsh* from this one historical event.

My argument, by contrast, is that the narrative tradition about the Battle of Carrhae, centering on a historical event, nevertheless fits a much older Iranian narrative tradition concerning the heroic conferral of *x^varənah*. Furthermore, as we will see, there are parallels in the Indic epic traditions.

In general, I follow Skjærvø in his "reflections on the question of how the oral tradition incorporated historical events and characters on one hand and foreign material on the other."[53] He gives a central illustration: "the example of Zarathustra and Vištāspa in Bactria and Babylon shows that the Old Iranian mythical and legendary characters <u>were repeatedly relocated in history</u> {83}."[54] We may start with Vištāspa: "What is surprising is that even such a 'recent' character as Darius' father Vištāspa seems to have retained none of his genuine historical identity, but has been completely integrated with the Vištāspa of the Young Avestan epic narratives."[55] Skjærvø then extends the argument to Zarathustra himself:

> By analogy with the case of Vištāspa we may wonder whether something similar may not have happened in the case of Zarathustra. The insistence of the sources in putting him either in Bactria or

49. Sarkārāti 1979–1977.
50. Alishan 1989:3.
51. Alishan 1989:5.
52. Alishan 1989:6.
53. Skjærvø 1996b:624; see also Skjærvø 1998b.
54. Skjærvø 1996b:624.
55. Skjærvø 1996b:624.

> Babylonia, combined with the uncertainty about the form of his name (Zathraustes, Zōroastrēs, Zaratas, Zaradēs), may well reflect some tradition by which a historical ruler was synchronized and identified with the Avestan Zarathustra, whom the oral poets and narrators then transported down in time and relocated.[56]

An important parallel to these Iranian typologies is the Indic typology of "partial incarnations."[57]

Similarly, my reading of the *Shāhnāma* reconstructs the epic role of Rostam as guardian of the Shāh's sovereignty back to the Iranian myths of Apąm Napāt as the rescuer of *x*ᵛ*arənah*. To repeat, this is not the same thing as to say that Rostam is Apąm Napāt.[58] Like Blois, Alishan misrepresents my argument: "Ultimately {84} Davidson's hypotheses [*sic*] argues for an identification [*sic*] of Rostam with the divinity Apām Napāt."[59]

Alishan claims that "Davidson does not distinguish between a god who keeps the *farr* in the absence of a legitimate ruler and the hero who protects the king (who already has the *farr* by the will of the celestial powers)."[60] In fact, I do systematically distinguish between god and hero, in terms of the various genres that represent them. In maintaining these distinctions, I am following Dumézil. By contrast, Alishan and Blois use the terms "god" and "hero" without distinguishing between the different genres that represent gods and heroes. Also, they ignore the argumentation in my 1985 article about the narrative parallelisms between gods in myth and heroes in epic, where I clearly follow the work of Dumézil, Puhvel, Watkins, and others on representations of the theme of dragon-killing in a variety of traditional genres.[61] In fact, both Alishan and Blois ignore all 1463 pages of Dumézil's *Mythe et épopée*. If nothing else, I hope that some day Alishan and Blois will read just four pages of Dumézil, *Mythe et épopée* 2.228–231, where he outlines the legacy of James Darmesteter[62] and Stig Wikander[63] in comparing the heroic traditions of the Iranian *Shāhnāma* and the Indic *Mahābhārata*.[64]

56. Skjærvø 1996b:626.

57. As mentioned by Skjærvø 1996b:626.

58. See also Davidson 2013a[1994]:106, with reference to Rostam in terms of Dumézil's typologies of heroes versus gods. Only in one context, p. 122, do I speak of Rostam and Apąm Napāt in terms of "is," and even then "only in earlier versions of the myth," and only in terms of Apąm Napāt as a heroic epithet.

59. Alishan 1989:6.

60. Alishan 1989:6. Both his qualifications—(1) about a "god" to whom *farr* defaults if the king is unworthy and (2) about the generic king as one "who already has the *farr* by the will of the celestial powers"—are tendentious and misleading.

61. Davidson 1985:120–126.

62. Darmesteter 1887.

63. Wikander 1959.

64. See also Skjærvø 1998b.

{85} Both Alishan and Blois mention Dumézil by name only, without citations of any of his publications, and only in the context of reproaching me for my reliance on his work. Their wording merits special attention.

First, Alishan: "Davidson's study, admirable in many other respects, suffers from one major flaw: the fallacy of approaching a subtle literary phenomenon such as the *Shāhnāmeh* with a preset formula or idea, be it Dumézil's, Wikander's, or her own."[65] Without making any invidious comparisons, I can only reply that Dumézil's work is sensitive to the subtle literary phenomena of convention and genre, and that his comparative as well as internal analysis of literary traditions—including classical Persian—stands on its own, hardly in need of any defense from me.

Then, Blois: "Davidson attempts to analyse the Iranian legend of the hero Rustam in the light of Dumézil's theory of the 'tripartite ideology of the Indo-Europeans', a theory which, for its part, has been the object of much learned criticism, notably in a lucid study of J. Brough in *BSOAS* 22 (1959),[66] pp. 69–85, and which has latterly come further into discredit after being adopted by the theoreticians of the self-styled 'new right' in French-speaking countries."[67] The arguments of Brough have been countered long ago by Dumézil,[68] and the substance of his counter-arguments stands, again, on its own.[69] Those who dismiss Dumézil's {86} work by reductionistically equating it with some vague theory about tripartite ideologies succeed only in proving that they do not really know the work of Dumézil, whose methods are consistently and rigorously based on the empirical details of text and language. Again I can say that Dumézil's work needs no defense from me.

The good name of Dumézil does need to be defended, however, against the innuendo in the wording of Blois about a "theory" that "has latterly come further into discredit after being adopted by the theoreticians of the self-styled 'new right' in French-speaking countries." To seek to discredit Dumézil's work by way of associating him, and, by implication, those who apply his methods and results, with adherents of what is vaguely described as the "new right" verges on behavior that is not only uncollegial but actionable. The wording of Blois evokes some of the negativity to be found in various earlier publications by other writers, some of whom have speculated that Dumézil sympathized with ultra-right theoreticians in the years leading up to the end of World War II. These speculations have been sys-

65. Alishan 1989:7. He gives no citations of Wikander's work, either. I assume that he means Wikander 1959. He concedes at p. 8n21: "My present critique shoud not imply that I fail to appreciate the range and profundity of Dumézil's extensive studies."

66. Brough 1959.

67. Blois 1998:269.

68. Dumézil 1959.

69. See further especially Dumézil 1968–1973:1.592–595, 3.342–361.

tematically documented, exposed, and refuted by Didier Eribon.[70] For a definitive and positive assessment of Eribon's book, I refer to the review of Pierre Vidal-Naquet.[71] The established credentials of Vidal-Naquet as a leading comparatiste, classicist, and historian of the Holocaust give added meaning to his resounding validation of the life and work of Dumézil.

The testimonial of Vidal-Naquet means a great deal to me personally, since it was he, along with Jean-Pierre Vernant, who {87} first introduced me to Dumézil in 1978 at the Collège de France in Paris. I say this not for the sake of "name-dropping"—returning one last time to a turn of phrase dear to Blois—but in order to put on record my own personal testimonial about Dumézil: in all my visits at 82 rue Notre Dame des Champs during the spring semesters of 1978 and 1982, he was for me a paragon of intellectual generosity and scholarly *humanitas*. At the time, I was a graduate student struggling to achieve a dissertation about the *Shāhnāma*, and I want to put it on record that Dumézil was for me the best teacher of comparative methodology.

I have no more to say about the general claims of Alishan and Blois against the applications of comparative evidence in studying the *Shāhnāma*. As for the specific claims of Alishan concerning the internal evidence of the *Shāhnāma*, I see additional problems. His arguments concerning specific contexts of *farr* in the *Shāhnāma* are unconvincing, since they are all based on his assumption that *farr* is inherent in kingship only, not in heroism.[72] This assumption renders his arguments circular.[73]

Before he finishes with me and with Dumézil, Alishan offers one last restatement of his pre-set ideas about "identification" {88} between god and hero: "Davidson's journey, as the title of her study indicates, begins with her misunderstanding of the concept of *tājbakhsh*."[74] After dismissing my 1985 work, which is actually named after the theme of the crown-bestower, Alishan launches into the second part of his article, starting afresh as if no one had ever written about this epithet: his first sentence reads: "It

70. Eribon 1992.

71. Vidal-Naquet 1992. See also the chapter "Dumézil rattrapé par la politique" in Coutau-Bégaire 1998:199–208.

72. Alishan 1989:6–7. He concedes (p. 6) that Rostam performs the function of bringing Key Qobād to power, but he claims that this function "is not the equivalent of conferring the *farr* on the king." When Key Kāʾus prays for divine forgiveness (*Shāhnāma* 2.155.441–457 Bertels), this act of repentance is for Alishan proof for his claim that Rostam's acknowledged function of bringing kings to power (or back to power) is not connected to *farr*.

73. The circularity verges on speciousness: commenting on the loss of *farr* by Key Kāʾus, and how this loss damages even Rostam's own realm, Alishan 1989:7 asks rhetorically: "is this the same Rostam who has the power to 'confer' *farr* upon Kayānid kings?"

74. Alishan 1989:8.

is a well-known but seldom-discussed fact that one of Rostam's epithets is *tājbakhsh*."[75]

Alishan's discussion is shaped by the assumption that specific episodes must have "inspired" the epithet *tājbakhsh*. In my work, by contrast, I follow the criteria of Milman Parry in stressing that such an epithet is not *generic* but *distinctive*.[76] For Parry, a distinctive epithet evolves out of traditional contexts that are suited to a specific entity.[77]

There are, in fact, numerous contexts in the *Shāhnāma* that suit the semantics of the epithet *tājbakhsh* as applying to Rostam. And yet, wherever Alishan finds contexts indicating that Rostam has the power to confer the crown upon the king, he resorts to special pleading in order to dismiss them. For example, in the passage where Key Qobād tells Rostam that he dreamt of two white falcons carrying the crown to him, and that Rostam is the realization of that dream (*Shāhnāma* 2.60.175–18 Bertels), Alishan argues that this passage {89} contains "spurious" verses, and the "original" variants do not justify the theme of conferring a crown.[78] Elsewhere, he dismisses as "scattered references" such related contexts as when Rostam promises that he will enthrone Esfandiyār "and place the crown upon his head personally,"[79] or when the hero promises Esfandiyār that he will enthrone and crown the prince Bahman (6.310.1480 Bertels).

Wherever the context of *tājbakhsh* does not refer explicitly to the conferring of a crown, Alishan dismisses it as "unroyal," as in the case of *Shāhnāma* 2.60.175–180 Bertels: "Ferdowsi has been obliged to introduce this epithet when Rakhsh sees Rostam struggling with the dragon, an event which takes place in a purely heroic and totally unroyal context."[80] In the end, Alishan concludes that the usage of the epithet *tājbakhsh* in the *Shāhnāma* is "not organic or integral" in its applications to Rostam.[81]

In his eagerness to explain the themes of *tājbakhsh* ultimately in terms of such historicized occasions as the crowning of the Parthian king by Surena,

75. Alishan 1989:9. At least Alishan acknowledges (p. 9n24) the seminal remarks of Maguire 1973:106–107 on the epithet *tājbakhsh*. I rely extensively on Maguire's work in Davidson 1985.

76. Davidson 2013a[1994]:4.

77. Parry 1971[1928] 156–157; cf. Nagy 1990a:33–34.

78. Alishan 1989:10, with bibliography on the claims for deeming this passage "spurious."

79. Alishan 1989:11, with reference to *Shāhnāma* 6.264.779 Bertels.

80. Alishan 1989:11; his assumption that this context is "unroyal" is unjustified. On the slaying of monsters, primarily "dragons," as a traditional function of heroes who protect kingship, see Watkins 1995, especially pp. 374–382; also pp. 314 and 316–317 on Thrita (where he distances himself from the theories of Boyce 1975–1982:1.85–108 concerning "real" *Āptii̯as supposedly living sometime before 2000 BCE). Cf. Puhvel 1987:112.

81. Alishan 1989:12.

Alishan goes out of his way to dissociate this epithet from the Iranian epic hero Rostam—just as he dissociates from Rostam the heroic role of maintaining the *farr* of the Shāh.

An egregious example is this claim about the hero Sām, the father of Rostam: "Sām's statement [of refusal to take over the {90} kingship of Shāh Nowzar, offered by dissatisfied Iranians] and his refusal of the crown *explicitly* refutes the idea that his family is in possession of the *farr-e shāhanshahi*."[82] I see here and elsewhere in Alishan's writings a basic misunderstanding of the theme inherent in the epithet *tājbakhsh*. The hero does not possess kingship in the sense that he is king, but in the sense that he is a kingmaker.

The epic function of Rostam and his lineage as kingmakers in the *Shāhnāma* of Ferdowsi is strikingly parallel to the function of Herakles in Greek epic traditions.[83] I have analyzed this aspect of the hero Herakles in an earlier work,[84] relying on the comparative material assembled by Dumézil in part 1 of volume 2 of his *Mythe et épopée*.[85] In the myths about Herakles, his status as the most powerful hero of his time is conventionally juxtaposed with his having to perform services to the king whose political power he sustains, his inferior cousin Eurystheus. This feature of the Greek hero Herakles, as an antagonistic subordinate of Eurystheus, is paralleled by the Old Norse hero Starkaðr and the Indic hero Śiśupāla:

> All three are kingmakers, not kings. That is, though they are constantly involved in the affairs of kings, they never aspire for kingship themselves. Starkaðr is in the service of several kings; Śiśupāla is the subordinate of Jarāsandha; and Herakles serves King Eurystheus throughout his Twelve Labors.[86]

{91} The objection may be raised that the parallelism of Rostam with Herakles is not complete: although Rostam is a political subordinate of the Shah, much like Herakles in relation to King Eurystheus, the Iranian hero is also a king in his own right—albeit a subordinate one. After all, the *Shāhnāma* of Ferdowsi makes it clear that Rostam is king over the remote frontier realm of Sistan. Even in this detail, however, he is parallel to other heroes in the Indo-European epic traditions. A case in point is the Greek hero Achilles, main hero of the Homeric *Iliad*. This brooding "loner" of a hero is in his own right a king, ruling over the remote realm of Phthia, and yet he is at the same time a political subordinate of King Agamemnon. This

82. Alishan 1989:7.
83. On Herakles in general, see again Watkins 1995:374–382.
84. Davidson 1980.
85. Dumézil 1968–1973:2.25–124.
86. Davidson 1980:199.

king, who "pulls rank" on Achilles in the celebrated provocation scene of Book 1 of the *Iliad*, is heroically inferior but politically superior to Achilles. And yet, Agamemnon's kingly power is consistently sustained by the heroic exploits of Achilles. Moreover, as I have shown in my earlier work, Homeric poetry in *Iliad* 19.95–133 explicitly compares the antagonistic but ultimately cooperative relationship between Achilles and Agamemnon to the relationship between Herakles and Eurystheus.[87]

In short, the role of Rostam as a "crown-bestower," *tājbakhsh*, of the Shāh fits the Indo-European model of a hero whose status as warrior sustains—albeit in a frequently antagonistic mode—the power and authority of the king. Dumézil describes this kind of epic relationship in terms of a stasis between *dux* and *rex*.[88] This {92} relationship, I argue, is built into the traditional epic contexts of the epithet *tājbakhsh*.[89]

There is comparative Iranian evidence for an analogous relationship in ceremonial or ritual contexts as well, going beyond the narrative about the crowning of the Parthian king by Surena in Plutarch *Life of Crassus* 21.6. In the inscription of the Sasanian king Narseh at Paikuli, composed in the early fourth century CE,[90] we may note the part of the narrative that concerns the accession of Narseh, the youngest son of Šābuhr I.[91] According to the narrative, Narseh was King of Armenia when the King of Kings, Warahrān II, son of Warahrān I, died. What happened next is summarized and discussed by Rahim Shayegan:

> [F]ollowing the death of the king of kings ... a certain Wahnām, son of Tadrōs (Tatrus), bestowed the crown upon Warahrān, king of Sakas, and son of the defunct King Warahrān II, without Narseh being informed of this succession:

87. Davidson 1980:200.

88. Dumézil 1968–1973:2.17–132.

89. Davidson 2013a[1994]:5, 10, 85–86, 88–90, 118–119, 144. Here and in my earlier discussion (1985), I pay special attention to representations of the hero Rostam as a political outsider, peripheral to the central kingdom, even though he is a narratological insider, central to the epic narratives about tensions between the "dux" and the "rex." I am therefore surprised at the claim of Alishan 1989:7–8n20: "It is not explained how Rostam could be Saka as an 'intrinsic' part of the Iranian national tradition." But I did explain in my work, as cited, and I did so at length. Alishan 1989:7–8n20 acknowledges, however, that my work does indeed take into account the various theories about Rostam's Saka "origin." On this topic, see especially Boyce 1955:475.

90. Edited by Humbach and Skjærvø 1978–1983.

91. I am grateful to Oktor Skjærvø and Rahim Shayegan for drawing my attention to this important piece of Iranian comparative evidence. On the oral heritage of Narseh's Paikuli inscription, see Skjærvø 1998c. For a recent and extensive study of the inscription, see Shayegan 2012, esp. ch. 6 (pp. 109–138).

> {93} ud Wahnām ī Tadrōsān [pad] xwēbeh drōžanīf (= the Parthian form) ud [pušt] ī Ahreman ud dēwān [pad Sagān šāh sar] dēhēm bandēd ud pad ān xīr nē amā ā[f]rāh kunēd
>
> And Wahnām, son of Tatrus, [through] his own falsehood and [with the help] of Ahriman and the devils [= *div*-s in Persian], attached the Diadem [to the head of Warahrān, king of Sakas]. And he did not inform us about the matter.[92]
>
> ... In Narseh's testimony, Wahnām's evil actions against the gods and the whole realm are attributed not only to the support of Ahreman and the devils (*[pad pušt] ī Ahreman ud dēwān*), but also to his own falsehood (*drōžanīh/ drōžanīf*) and sorcery (*jādūgīh*), which rendered him a follower of Lie (*drōzan/drō an*), i.e., a usurper.[93] ... [Warahrān] is never directly accused of falsehood and treachery. Moreover, it appears that it is merely his association with the principal villain, the crown-bestower Wahnām, who used sorcery to put him on the throne, that delegitimizes his rule.[94]

At a later point in the narrative, the nobles of 'the Persians and Parthians' (*Pārsān ud Pahlawān*) are informed, in direct quotation, that '[I, Wahnām, son of Tatrus have] attached the Diadem to the head of [Warahrān] king of Sakas', and the expression is *dēhēm* (*bandēm*), corresponding to the expression *dēhēm bandēd* 'he attached the Diadem' in the earlier part of the narrative.[95]

One major question remains: can we find comparative Indo-European evidence for the actual gesture of bestowing a crown? Decisive information comes from the vast body of documentation concerning an ancient Indic royal consecration ritual known as the *rājasūya*.[96]

{94} Although there is no direct parallel featuring a "crown" in the Indic *rājasūya*, there are numerous indirect parallels featuring other regal paraphernalia as conferred by officiants at the consecration ritual.[97] So long as such paraphernalia serve the function of indicating the radiant authority

92. Shayegan 2012:109.

93. Shayegan 2012:113; emphasis mine.

94. Shayegan 2012:119–120; emphasis mine.

95. Shayegan 2012:126.

96. I rely on the standard work concerning the *rājasūya*, Heesterman 1957. See also the essential supplements in Witzel 1987.

97. Among such officiants are the *ratnin*-s, "members of the royal household, bearers of royal treasures" (Heesterman 1957:49). "The *ratnin* episode [of the *rājasūya* ritual] is one of the few parts of the *rājasūya* that are directly and exclusively related to kingship" (p. 50). According to the *Taittirīya Brāhmaṇa* (1.7.3.1), the *ratnin*-s are the givers and takers of the realm (*pradātāraḥ*; *apadātāraḥ*); in the ritual formula, "they extend to him [the king] the realm" (pp.50–51).

that is being conferred ritually on the king, they may be considered parallels to the "crown" that is being conferred—narratologically—on the Shāh.

One such regal object in the Indic ritual of the *rājasūya* is a gold plaque with a hundred perforated holes that notionally radiate outward the inner charisma of the inaugurated king. This gold plaque is held over the head of the sacrificer as king: "The holes in the plaque placed on the head of the sacrificer are intended to let the unction fluid flow through; flowing through the holes in the gold plaque the unction fluid becomes *āyuṣya-* and *varcasya-*, thus imparting force and lustre (*āyus-* and *varcas-*) to the sacrificer."[98] The semantics of Vedic *āyus-* 'force' and *varcas-* 'lustre' are directly {95} comparable with those of Avestan *x*ᵛ*arənah*.[99] The gold sheet known as the *paṭṭa* is actually bound on the king's forehead, and this binding is the ritual act of "crowning."[100]

Another aspect of the *rājasūya* ritual is the "purification of the waters," which is linked with Apām Napāt: "The 'purification' of the waters seems to refer to the cosmic process of the igneous principle entering into a union with the aquatic principle to be reborn from it: Apām Napāt, ... who is invoked together with the divine female waters at the drawing of the waters, is identical with Agni. The same idea seems also to be applied to Agni's celestial form, the sun, who, hidden in the Ocean, was raised from it by the gods."[101]

At the so-called *mahābhiṣeka* 'big *abhiṣeka* (unction)' of Indra described in the *Aitareya Brāhmaṇa* (8.17.5), the 'kingmakers' (*rājakartr̥-*) acclaim the king with the words: 'the royal power has been born, the *kṣatriya* [warrior] has been born, the overlord of all being has been born, the eater of the people has been born, the slayer of the enemies has been born, the protector of the brahmins has been born, the protector of the cosmic order has been born.'[102]

98. Heesterman 1957:112–113, 149. On the semantic overlap of king and sacrificer, see Heesterman p. 149n40, with reference to *pūrvāgni-* as a "fossil" in the *rājasūya*: "This case may be cited as an instance of the development of the Vedic ritual through the extension and systemization of the royal cities. In the course of this process the king was generalized into a common sacrificer and finally the royal rites were incorporated in the extended and elaborated Soma ritual, which itself represents a development from the royal ritual." See also Heesterman p. 227 on the generalizing of the king into the *yajamāna* 'sacrificer.'

99. Witzel 1987:455 explicitly compares the Vedic concepts of ritual radiance at the *rājasūya* with Avestan *x*ᵛ*arənah*.

100. Witzel 1987:421, 425, 455, 459–460, with a clear analysis of the homology between the *paṭṭa* and our notions of 'crown.'

101. Heesterman 1957:87–88. Note too pp. 168–170, on the sacrifice to Apām Napāt (among others) at the end of unction.

102. Heesterman 1957:117, with this comment at 117n20: "This acclamation is performed between the enthronement and the unction proper." See also pp. 117–118: "that the unction

{96} Aside from the ritual details of the Indic *rājasūya* that express the idea of kingship, we must also consider the ritual participants themselves. How are we to imagine a "crown-bestower" in terms of the *rājasūya*? Of particular interest is the narration of a *rājasūya* in the Indic epic tradition, in the *Mahābhārata*, 2[25–26] 33–42. I stress an essential narrative detail: Yudhiṣṭhira, as king, is being officially inaugurated at his *rājasūya* by Kṛṣṇa, who is explicitly described in this context as a warrior or *kṣatriya* (2[25] 35).[103] In Dumézil's terms, it is a *dux* who is bestowing kingship on the *rex*.[104] Moreover, in the same epic context, Kṛṣṇa is challenged by a rival *dux*, Śiśupāla, whose own *rex* is the chief rival of Yudhiṣṭhira.[105] Śiśupāla describes Kṛṣṇa explicitly as a non-king and as one who is therefore undeserving of the honors that Kṛṣṇa receives at the *rājasūya* (2[25] 34). As soon as Śiśupāla is killed by Kṛṣṇa, a fiery light, *tejaḥ*, which is compared to the sun, leaves his body and is miraculously absorbed by the body of his killer (2[26] 42). Once Śiśupāla is killed, the consecration of Yudhiṣṭhira as king finally takes place, who then declares to Kṛṣṇa that it is by his grace that the ritual has been accomplished.[106]

This example from Indic epic provides a most precious piece of comparative evidence for understanding the function of Rostam as a bestower of kingship. Iranian epic, as I noted earlier, expresses {97} the idea of a hero's conferring kingship only narratologically, not ritually. In the case of this passage from the *Mahābhārata* the expression is simultaneously ritual and narratological. I propose that we can reconstruct a parallel ritual dimension in the function of Rostam as *tājbakhsh* 'crown-bestower.'

This proposal of mine gains tripodal stability in light of the fact that Greek mythology offers a *tertium comparationis* to the Indic and Iranian evidence. In a narrative that is best represented by Ode 17 of Bacchylides, the hero Theseus participates in a series of events that combine the inherited tradition of a brilliant, fiery 'descendant of the waters' with the receipt of royal insignia. According to Bacchylides' ode, our hero is on board the ship that is to convey to the Minotaur the adolescents with whom Minos annually requires the Athenians to sate the monstrous appetite of his wife Pasiphae's semi-taurine son, whom Theseus intends to defeat. (And in so doing, Theseus will save his fellow adolescents.) Minos himself is also on

---

rite under discussion [*abhiṣeka*] represents the new birth is already suggested by the word *rājasūya* ('bringing forth the king')." On Indra as a model for the king, see Heesterman p. 225.

103. On the Indo-European background of Kṛṣṇa see Puhvel 1987:56, 71, 77–83, 87–90, 92, 247–250; cf. also Dumézil 1968–1973:2.60n1.

104. Dumézil 1968–1973:2.59–116. See also Davidson 1980.

105. Cf. also Dumézil 1968–1973:2.66 on the function of Śiśupāla as the *senāpatiḥ* 'commander of the armies.'

106. Cf. Dumézil 1968–1973:2.60.

board the ship, and incites Theseus to prove that he is the son of Poseidon by retrieving a gleaming golden ring that Minos has tossed overboard. Theseus accepts the challenge and dives down to the depths of the Aegean. Having arrived at Poseidon's submarine abode, he encounters the Nereids, from whose limbs, Bacchylides tells us, shines a σέλας | ὧτε πυρός "radiance like fire" (104–105), and whose heads are bound with golden fillets (105–107). Theseus then meets a particular Nereid, his mother Amphitrite, whose golden veil the hero mentioned to Minos just before plunging into the sea in pursuit of the golden ring (36–38).

And now the moment that is especially significant for my argument: Amphitrite wraps Theseus in a purple robe and sets a *plókos* 'wreath' upon his head (112–114). Bacchylides describes this wreath as ῥόδοις ἐρεμνόν "dark with roses" (116), the opacity of which we might interpret as the poet's elegant inversion of the thematic luminosity with which his composition has been characterized up until now. In fact other authors describe Amphitrite's wreath as golden (Pausanias 1.17.3) and sparkling with gemstones (Hyginus *Poeticon Astronomicon* 2.5). So, from a diachronic perspective, we may understand this manifestation of royal insignia as yet another example of the recurring luminous leitmotif that runs throughout the narrative. In any event, Theseus emerges from the sea miraculously dry and dressed in these tokens of his divine parentage, and in so doing proves that Poseidon is his father, indeed confirming that he is none other than a 'descendant of the waters'.

Allowing for many discrepancies, the narrative of Theseus' submarine descent and subsequent emergence shares a number of structural components and thematic elements with that of Fraŋrasiian's attempt to obtain the *x^varənah* following its seizure by Apąm Napāt.[107] To be sure, what is immediately at stake in Ode 17 of Bacchylides is not the acquisition of kingly authority, but rather the confirmation of parentage. We might simply invoke the phenomenon that Dumézil called a *glissement fonctionnel*. Or we might rather observe that in proving his divine paternity to the skeptical Minos, Theseus compromises Minos' tyrannical authority, as he continues to do by slaying the Minotaur and by eloping with Minos' daughter Ariadne. So the events of Ode 17 of Bacchylides seem to be bound up with an effort to contrast the illegitimate sovereign Minos with the heroic Theseus, determined to protect the Athenian adolescents.[108] To resume the Dumézilian

107. As noted above, the correspondences were first substantially demonstrated by Louden 1999, but anticipated to a certain extent by Gershenson 1991:87–88. Louden's analysis has recently been endorsed by West 2007:270–2.

108. Cf. Louden 1999, esp. 63–64, 75–76, who characterizes the hostility between Theseus and Minos as reflecting a primarily political struggle.

dyad discussed above, it is as though Theseus in his capacity as champion of the Athenian adolescents functions as the *dux* of his mortal father, the Athenian *rex* Aegeus, who has been compelled by Minos to sacrifice to the Minotaur youths from his own domain.[109] With respect to Minos' initial gesture, Bruce Louden argues that although in synchronic terms Minos tosses his golden ring into the sea willingly, from a diachronic point of view this gesture might be said to represent the departure from a deficient monarch of the luminous essence that authorizes the dominion of Indo-European kings, much in the same way as the submarine *xᵛarənah* leaps away from the grasp of Fraŋrasiian, who is unworthy of receiving it.[110]

With an eye to the structural and thematic correspondences between the conflict of Theseus and Minos in Bacchylides 17 and the actions of the *xᵛarənah*, of Apąm Napāt, and of Apąm Napāt's rival Fraŋrasiian in *Yašt* 19, it becomes significant for the present essay that Rostam, the enemy of Fraŋrasiian's epic correlate Afrāsiyāb, is associated not only with the establishment of legitimate kingly authority in general, but that in his epithet *tājbakhsh* 'crown-bestower' he is also associated in particular with a specific object of regalia indicative of such sanctioned authority. Surely it is no coincidence that in a Greek narrative cognate with that of *Yašt* 19, which is in turn the Avestan narrative equivalent to Rostam's micro-narrative epithet *tājbakhsh* 'crown-bestower', the goddess Amphitrite decorates Theseus' head with a *plókos* 'wreath', which is *mutandis mutandis* a crown. If we validate this comparison, it emerges that an object of royal headgear was already a fixture of the Indo-European narrative complex that informs both the Greek narrative and the Persian micro-narrative under scrutiny.[111]

In terms of Persian epic, however, what is ultimately at stake is not kingship per se but the charisma that comes with kingship—a charisma derived from heroic radiance. That radiance is *xᵛarənah* or *farr*. That radiance, moreover, is not only heroic: it is thereby also inherently poetic.[112] That *farr*, I submit, is what radiates from Ferdowsi's *Book of Kings*.

109. Note that in Theseus' role of *dux* for Aegeus, who is both the hero's *rex* and his father, we have yet another intersection of paternity and royalty.

110. Louden 1999:66.

111. My analysis of the Greek comparanda is strongly influenced by the advice of John McDonald.

112. For a demonstration, by way of Irish parallels, see Ford 1974.

Essay Six

Epic as a Frame for Speech-Acts

Ritual Boasting in the *Shāhnāma* of Ferdowsi[1]

{99} This essay builds on the new methodology developed by Richard P. Martin concerning the phenomenon of "embedded genres" within epic. In his detailed study of the Homeric *Iliad*, Martin shows that ancient Greek epic has the capacity of embedding or framing, within itself, various kinds of speech-acts such as boasting, praising, blaming, threatening, prophesying, lamenting.[2] The comparative ethnographic evidence adduced by Martin shows that such speech-acts could be "genres" in their own right outside of epic, but inside of epic they become "sub-genres" that follow not only their own internal rules but also the external rules of the genre that contains them, epic. In this essay I will concentrate on the conventions of heroic boasting as "quoted" by epic. My examples will be taken from the Persian national epic, the *Shāhnāma* of Ferdowsi.

In studying the phenomenon of ritual boasting as represented by Persian epic, I will apply the methods developed by Leonard C. Muellner in his study of the sub-genre of boasting as framed by the genre of archaic Greek epic.[3] As Muellner shows, the phenomenon of ritual boasting as represented by the Homeric *Iliad* and *Odyssey* {100} is not just a poetic representation. The boasts of heroes, framed by epic, follow the distinct rules of a sub-genre within epic.[4]

When a Homeric hero boasts, he not only "means it:" he is expressing himself in the society's most sanctioned mode of speech.[5] The importance of

1. This essay develops ideas explored in Davidson 1998a.

2. Martin 1989. For an anthropological application of the concept of "speech-act," see Martin pp. 12, 21–22, 31–32, 52, going beyond the hypothetical applications of Austin 1962 and of Searle 1979.

3. Muellner 1976. For the importance of this work in exploring methods of "recapturing the semantics of words for speech when we have no native informants and only poetic texts," see Martin 1989:12.

4. For more on the term "sub-genre," see Muellner 1976:32n32: "To conceive of the Epic genre as containing a series of sub-genres seems an effective way to account for the isolation of thematic and linguistic phenomena in specific contexts."

5. See especially Muellner 1976:78.

boasting in the society represented by epic, and the status of boasting as a speech-act in that society, is dramatized by the epic narrative that "quotes" the boasts. When a hero boasts, he formally identifies his status—even his "role"—in epic narrative. In other words, the performative aspects of a hero's self-identification are treated by epic as a specially privileged statement of the truth as seen by epic.[6] Further, the sub-genre of boasting is closely related to the sub-genre of praising. The truth-value of boasting, delivered in the first person, corresponds to the truth-value of praising, delivered in the second person, and both are framed by the truth-value of epic narrating, delivered in the third person.[7]

As with the first-person activity of boasting, the second-person activity of praising is not just a poetic representation in epic. The praising of heroes by other heroes, as "quoted" by epic, follows the distinct rules of another sub-genre within epic. Moreover, this sub-genre of praise, as framed by Homeric poetry, is clearly cognate with the genre of praise poetry, which is independently attested in {101} archaic Greek poetic traditions, most notably in the victory odes of Pindar.[8] Symmetrically, the sub-genre of blame or invective, as framed by Homeric poetry in dramatized situations where one hero hurls invectives against another, is cognate with the genre of blame poetry, which is also independently attested in archaic Greek poetic traditions, for example in the lampoons of Archilochus.[9] It can even be argued that "Greek epic presents its own genesis in terms of the opposition between praise and blame."[10]

In archaic Greek epic, the narration and "quotation" of boasting by heroes is only one side of the picture: the other side is the insulting of these heroes by rival heroes, which is also narrated and "quoted" by epic. Richard Martin analyzes the "boast and insult contests" dramatized by Homeric poetry, comparing a corresponding form in Scandinavian poetics, *flyting*.[11] As Martin points out, there is even a formal study that compares the Scandinavian institution of the flyting with dramatized quarrel scenes in archaic Greek epic.[12]

6. Muellner 1976:78, 99, analyzes the semantics of Homeric *eukhomai* (the textbook translation for which is 'boast') as 'say (proudly, accurately, contentiously)'.

7. On epic as a third-person frame for second-person speech-acts of praise, see Nagy 1990b:150, 197.

8. See Nagy 1990b, especially ch. 6 ("Epic, Praise and the Possession of Poetry").

9. See Nagy 1999a[1979], especially ch. 12 ("Poetry of Praise, Poetry of Blame"), ch. 13 ("Iambos"), and ch. 14 ("Epos, the Language of Blame, and the Worst of the Achaeans").

10. Nagy 1990a:17, with reference to the Judgment of Paris retelling in *Iliad* 24.

11. Martin 1989:47; see his extended analysis at pp. 68–77.

12. Martin 1989:68n44, with reference to Parks 1986. See now Parks 1990, especially p. 196n4.

The institution of "boast and insult contests" or "verbal duels," as we shall see, is also reflected in the quarrel scenes of Persian epic. Applying Martin's methods, I will focus on one particular verbal duel, the quarrel between the heroes Rostam and Esfandiyār, which will eventually escalate into physical combat on the battlefield—a struggle that Rostam will win when he kills {102} Esfandiyār.[13] This physical combat, the object of which is to determine which of the combatants is the better hero, is actually prefigured by their verbal combat, which has the same object. Here too I will apply the methods of Martin, who shows that Homeric struggles over who is the best hero imply a parallelism between the ideas of best warrior and best speaker:

> Does Homer depict one hero as a better speaker? If so, how can we tell? The answers would have to come from literary stylistics. Thus far, no method has been found to support an answer. But a naive audience, taking mimesis at face value, might ask: Is one hero a better speaker? I suggest that a traditional oral-poetic audience is "naive" inasmuch as it has internalized the conventions of the overarching genre (in this case, epic) to the extent that it can focus more than we can on the primary, subgeneric level, on what a hero says and does, and, most important, how he does it. I am adopting this "naive" view because I believe that the taxonomy of speech terms has given us a native, internal insight into what constitutes important heroic speech. And this view, I suggest, actually pays more attention to style than does a more "literary" analysis, as the "naive" listener of the *Iliad* assumes that individual speakers—in poems or in the world at large—have an inherent "style"; it is not (as criticism has often treated it) something imposed by an "author". Heroes are their own authors, performers in every sense."[14]

{103} In what follows, I will apply Martin's methods by focusing on the subgeneric level of the verbal duel between Rostam and Esfandiyār in the *Shāhnāma*. Also, I propose to apply the terms "tenor" and "vehicle" respectively to the framing narrative of epic and to the framed verbal duel that is "quoted" by the narrative.[15] Using these terms, I ask the question: how does

13. I follow in general the readings found in Mohl 1838–1878:4.600–634.1200–1460. The more "scientific" Moscow edition of the *Shāhnāma* omits, on the basis of editorial assumptions with which I do not agree (see Essay Two), a number of the verses included by Mohl (Bertels *et al.* 1960–1971:6.254–70). On the editorial assumptions of the "scientific" editions, see Davis 1995b, esp. p. 395.

14. Martin 1989:90. This insight about "heroes as performers" has been applied to living oral epic traditions by Reynolds 1995, especially p. 207. See further in Essay Seven.

15. The terms (1) "vehicle" and (2) "tenor," referring respectively to (1) a simile or metaphor and (2) a narrative that contains that simile or metaphor, goes back to I. A. Richards

the vehicle of the sub-genre of the verbal duel that is framed (or "quoted") by epic affect the tenor of the epic narrative that frames (or "quotes") it?[16]

In this verbal duel between Rostam and Esfandiyār, each of the two heroes boasts about himself in the first person and insults the other in the second person, using conventions of blame-poetry in the second person. Both heroes temper their blame poetics with praise poetics, again in the second person. The third-person narrative of epic records these second-person expressions of praise and blame, juxtaposing them with the first-person expressions of self-praise, that is, boasting. After "quoting" this combat in words of praise and blame between the two heroes, the epic proceeds to narrate the physical combat that follows, in which Rostam wins by killing Esfandiyār.

As we join the narrative, we find the warrior-prince Esfandiyār pressing his quest to humiliate the warrior Rostam in public by {104} binding him and dragging him back to Shāh Goshtāsp. The stakes are very high. Throughout the *Shāhnāma* the hero Rostam has been the *pahlavān-e jahan* 'champion of the world', serving capricious *shāh*-s, making extreme personal sacrifices for country and throne, in order to keep the *shāh* on the throne and Iran safe from chaos. Shāh Goshtāsp, by sending out his son Esfandiyār to bind Rostam in order to humiliate him, has created a crisis for both Rostam and Esfandiyār. Esfandiyār knows that this demand is outrageous—and yet he must obey or else be accused of insurrection. Rostam, on the other hand, cannot bow to this humiliation because the degradation would cancel his former glory, as narrated by the epic that frames his identity.

Before the two heroes are pitted against each other in battle, the tensions of the heroic crisis are played out in the narrative framework of a sumptuous feast to be attended by Rostam and Esfandiyār, which will serve as the setting for their verbal duel. Since Esfandiyār is the outsider who has entered Rostam's territory, it is up to Rostam to show him hospitality by providing a feast in his honor. Esfandiyār, however, exercises his role as future *shāh* and feastgiver by insisting that he give the feast. Already there is a conflict of status, since both are vying over who gets to have the upper hand in taking an initiative.

In recognition of his social superiority, Esfandiyār is ceded the right to give the feast. Then, in order to show how much he is in control, Esfandiyār deliberately neglects to invite Rostam, who is thus forced to come uninvited

---

1936:90 and following. For an important new method in applying these old terms, see Muellner 1990.

16. For more on the notion of sub-genre as "vehicle," see Muellner 1990:60n1.

to the feast, demanding to know why {105} he is being slighted.[17] As Rostam the Warrior approaches Prince Esfandiyār's camp, the prince's men seem to recognize the warrior's superiority as warrior when they gaze at him:

همی گفت لشکر که این نامدار   نماند بکس جز بسام سوار
بر آن کوهۀ زین که آهنست   همان رخش گویی که آهرمنست
اگر همنبردش بود ژنده پیل   برافشان تو بر تارک پیل نیل
خرد نیست اندر سر شهریار   که با فّرگردی چو اسفندیار
بدینسان همی از پی تاج و گاه   بکشتن دهد نامداری چو ماه
بپیری سوی گنج یازانتراست   بمهر و بدیهیم نازانتراست

Mohl 4.608.2972–7[18]

The army said all at once that this famed one
resembles none other than Sām, the horseman.

Upon that saddlecloth he is iron,
so too one might say that Rakhsh[19] is Ahriman.

If his battle foe is a huge elephant,
the skull of that elephant, as with dye of indigo, will be shattered.

{106} There is no wise judgement inside the head of the ruler,
when he allows such a *farr*-winning one as Esfandiyar,

in this way, ever for the sake of crown and throne,
to be destroyed—the fame of such a moon.

With old age he [= the Shāh Goshtāsp] is ever more desirous of the
hoarding of treasure,
with his seal and the jewel-encrusted crown he is ever more vainglorious.[20]

In this way, epic is already validating the outcome of the verbal combat that will follow during the feast.

In the setting of the feast, the heroes' first-person boastings about their martial feats mirror the third-person epic narratives about these same feats.

17. For an analogous theme in the archaic Greek epic tradition, see the Proclus summary of the Epic *Cypria* (Allen 1902–1912:5.104.23–24): Achilles has a quarrel with Agamemnon over not being invited on time to a feast (cf. the comments in Nagy 1999a[1979]:23).

18. Here and elsewhere in this essay, I cite the line-numbers according to Mohl's edition (see note above).

19. Rostam's steed.

20. The *Shāhnāma* frequently contrasts the idle luxuriance of unjust *shāh*-s with the warrior ethic of Rostam: see Davis 1992.

For example, one of Esfandiyār's greatest epic moments is his exploit in capturing the Brazen Hold. In the context of his verbal duel with Rostam, he refers to that epic narrative in the format of a first-person boast:

چونان‌خورده‌شد‌جام‌می‌را‌بخواست   زرویین دژ آنگه سخن کرد راست
وزان مردی خود همی کرد یاد   بیاد شهنشاه می خورد شاد

Mohl 4.608.2960–1

When the bread was consumed he [Esfandiyār] asked for a goblet {107} of wine
and told about the Brazen Hold,

and he at once recollected his own manliness
and made merry toasts to the Shāhanshāh.

In response to this first-person re-performance by Esfandiyār of his own epic, Rostam combines the first-person poetics of boasting with the second-person poetics of blame as he addresses Esfandiyār:

نگهدار شاهان و ایران منم   بهر جای پشت دلیران منم
ازین خواهش من شدی در گمان   مدان خویشرا برتر از آسمان

Mohl 4.610.2990–2991

I am the guardian of kings and of Iran,
I am the buttress of all the valiant ones.

You have become doubtful of this proposal of mine.
Don't believe yourself to be higher than the heavens.

Esfandiyār affirms that he deliberately did not invite Rostam. But before the verbal combat becomes prematurely overheated, Esfandiyār then makes a gesture at cooling things down by saying to Rostam:

شدی تنگدل چون نیامد خرام   نجستم همی زین سخن کام و نام
چنین گرم شد روز و راه دراز   نکردم ترا رنجه تندی مساز

Mohl 4.610.3001–2

{108} You became upset when my hospitality was not forthcoming.
I was not seeking to find[21] in these words my valor and fame.

The day was hot and the road was long.
I did not want to vex you. Do not be angry.

21. Here I follow the manuscript reading adopted in the Moscow edition.

During this interlude of "cooling off," Esfandiyār mixes in words of praise for Rostam by saying that he has heard about the hero from *mōbad*-s. Throughout the *Shāhnāma*, the epic refers to *mōbad*-s as generic performers of epic.[22] Thus the second-person words of praise recapitulate the third-person words of epic narrative that *mōbad*-s would perform. Nevertheless, almost in the same breath, Esfandiyār's words switch from the second-person poetics of praise to the second-person poetics of blame, in that he interprets the words of the *mōbad*-s in a negative light, impugning the genealogy of Rostam:

چنین گفت با رستم اسفندیار   که ای نیکدل مهتر نامدار
من ایدون شنیدستم از موبدان   بزرگان و بیدار دل بخردان
که دستان بد گوهر از دیوزاد   بگیتی فزون زین ندارد نژاد
فراوان زسامش نهان داشتند   همی رستخیز جهان داشتند

Mohl 4.612.3016–19

{109} Thus Esfandiyār said to Rostam
O good-hearted, famous lord,

I had heard thus from the *mōbad*-s,
the great ones and attentive-hearted wise ones,

that Dastān[23] of evil stock was born from a *div*[24]
and in the world his pedigree did not have anything higher than this.[25]

They for a long time kept him hidden from Sām,
they were holding back the turmoil for the world.

Esfandiyār goes on to boast that his ancestors materially provided for the father of Rostam:

خجسته بزرگان و شاهان من   نیاگان من نیکخواهان من
ورا بر کشیدند و دادند چیز   فراوان بدین سال بگذشت نیز

Mohl 4.614.3029–30

My blessed elders and my kings,
my grandsires and well-wishers,

22. For more on references in the *Shāhnāma* to the *mōbad* (and to the *dehqān*) as a generic performer of epic, see Essay Three, with reference to Davidson 2013a[1994]:29–33.
23. Dastān is an alternative name for Zāl, Rostam's father.
24. A *div* is a 'demon' in the Zoroastrian world-view.
25. That is, his social status could not move upward.

brought him up and gave him things
in abundance, as the years passed by.

{110} These words of blame, impugning the genealogy of Rostam, give the hero his opportunity to perform his epic genealogy in the first person, as a boast, and he proceeds to do so in detail at Mohl 4.614.3036 and following. Before Rostam begins his boast, however, he praises Esfandiyār as someone who knows by heart all of epic tradition—and then uses that praise to turn around and blame him for not performing the epic theme of Rostam correctly, as it were:

بدو گفت رستم که ای یادگیر   چه گویی سخنهای نا دلپذیر
دلت پیش کژی بنالد همی   روانت ز دیوان ببالد همی

Mohl 4.614.3034–5

Rostam said to him [= Esfandiyār]: "O you storehouse of memories,
Why utter speech not amiable?

Your heart always grieves over crookedness,
but your soul always waxes great with demons [*div*-s]."

In other words, if you are so devoted to combatting incorrectness, like the incorrectness of demons who are the enemies of Zoroastrian thought, why is it that you are incorrect about my epic reputation?

Rostam then proceeds to boast: that is, he retells, in the first person, his greatest moments (so far) in epic:

نه ارژنگ ماندم نه دیو سفید   نه سنجه نه اولاد غندی نه بید
همان از پی شاه فرزند را   بکشتم دلیر خردمند را
که گردی چو سهراب دیگر نبود   بزور و بمردی و رزم آزمود

{111} Mohl 4.616.3059–3061

I left alive neither Arzhang, nor the White Div,
nor Sanjah, nor the Awlād Ghandi, nor Bid.

And, following in the footsteps of the Shāh,
I killed my own son, the valiant one, the wise one.

There was no one like Sohrāb
in strength, manliness, and battle skills.

Rostam also catalogues his chief attributes as an epic hero:

که من بودم اندر جهان کامران   مرا بود شمشیر و گرزگران

Mohl 4.616.3069

since I have been blessed within this world
I have a sword and heavy mace.

Proceeding to blame Esfandiyār for temporarily forgetting his knowledge of epic because of his own self-absorption, Rostam slows down the pace of the verbal duel by saying that he is ready to drink wine as a lubricant for further boasting:

تن خویش بینی همی در جهان   نه ای آگه از کارهای نهان {112}
چو بسیار شد گفتها می خورم   بمی جان اندیشه را بشکرم

Mohl 4.616.3072–3

You see only your own self in this world,
and you are unaware of its secret workings.

Since there is a plethora of talking, I now drink wine;
with wine I will sweeten the anxieties of the soul.

In the relaxed atmosphere of the feast, Esfandiyār allows himself to acknowledge Rostam's epic reputation:

بدو گفت کز رنج و پیکار تو   شنیدم همه درد و تیمار تو

Mohl 4.618.3075

He [= Esfandiyār] said to him [= Rostam]: "I have heard about all your troubles and combats, all of your pains and sorrows."

What is even more remarkable, the warrior-prince Esfandiyār acknowledges his own conflicts with royalty:

وز آنپس که مارا بگفت گرزم   ببستم پدر دور کردم ز بزم
بلهراسپ از بند من بد رسید   شد از ترک روی زمین ناپدید

Mohl 4.618.3094–5

{113} And after that, acting on the words that Gorazm spoke about me,
my father bound me and kept me far from the feast.

The evil of my being bound affected Lohrāsp
and the face of the earth was overrun by Turkoman hordes.

Then Esfandiyār proceeds to boast of his own heroic deeds, thereby retelling his own epic narrative. He refers to these deeds as *Haft Khwān*, meaning 'seven banquet-courses', which is the conventional epic way to designate the seven most celebrated heroic adventures of Esfandiyār—and of Rostam.[26] With this designation *Haft Khwān*, Persian epic indicates the context as well as the content of epic performance: the primary setting for the narration of epic, according to this designation, is the banquet or feast.[27] In the present context, where the two heroes of *Haft Khwān* epic traditions are having a real *khwān* or 'feast' with each other, the warrior-prince Esfandiyār can narrate his own epic in the form of a boast:

شنیدی که در هفتخوان پیش من   چو آمد ز دیوان آن انجمن
بچاره برویین دژ اندر شدم   جهانی بر آنگونه بر هم زدم
بجستم همی کین ایرانیان   بخون بزرگان ببستم میان

Mohl 4.620.3103–5

You heard that in my *Haft Khwān*,
and what befell me from *div*-s of that ilk.

{114} By a trick I entered the Brazen Hold
and dashed together a world in this manner.

I set upon avenging the Iranians,
for the blood of the Elders I girded my waist.

یکی تیره دژ بر سر کوه بود   که از برتری دور از انبوه بود

Mohl 4.620.3108

There was a dark castle on top of the mountain
which, in its height, was far from the crowd of men.

برافروختم آتش زردهشت   که با مجمر آورده بود از بهشت
بپیروزی داد گر یک خدای   بایران چنان آمدم باز جای

Mohl 4.620.3112–3

I lit the fire of Zardhusht [= Zoroaster]
which in a censer [*mijmar*] was brought from Paradise.

26. On the *Haft Khwān* 'seven banquet-courses' epic traditions of Esfandiyār and Rostam, see Essay Two above, with reference to Davidson 2013a[1994]:138–148, which includes material previously explored in Davidson 1990. See also Davidson 2002.

27. Davidson 2013a[1994]:138–148.

With the victories owed to the just and only God
thus I returned once again to Iran.

We have seen here an overwhelming array of Esfandiyār's greatest epic moments and heroic attributes. At a later point, the prince refers to perhaps the single most distinctive detail about his epic {115} essence:

چو من زین زرین نهم بر سیاه   بسر بر نهم خسروانی کلاه

Mohl 4.624.3153

When I place a golden saddle[28] upon the dark steed
and wear the royal crown upon my head.

In response to Esfandiyār's boasts as "performed" from his epic *Haft Khwān* repertoire, Rostam proceeds to boast by "performing" from his own *Haft Khwān*:

مرا یار در هفت خوان رخش بود   کجا زور سمش جهانبخش بود

Mohl 4.622.3124

Rakhsh was my helper in the *Haft Khwān*—
whose hooves have the strength to bestow a whole world.

But then, Rostam's boasting or first-person praise modulates into second-person blame of Esfandiyār:

وگر نه کجا بود تاج شما   همان یاره و تخت عاج شما
تو اندر جهان پهلوان نوی   نو آیین واز تخم کیخسروی {116}
من از کودکی تا شدستم کهن   ازین گونه از کس نبودم سخن

Mohl 4.622.3137–9

If not here [i.e. if I were not here], where would your crown be,
or your necklace, or your ivory throne?

You are a new hero in this world
with new customs and from the seed of Key Khosrow.

Since my youth until my becoming old
no one has spoken to me in this manner.

28. On references to the saddles of Esfandiyār and Rostam in earlier Iranian epic traditions (e.g. the *Draxt Asūrik*), see Davidson 2013a[1994]:82.

The good cheer of the feast is giving way, inevitably, to the doom of the physical combat that will follow the verbal combat:[29]

اگر بر چنین روی گردد سپهر   بپوشد میان دو تن روی مهر
بجای می سرخ کین آوریم   کمان و کمند کمین آوریم
غوکوس خواهیم ز آوای رود   بتیغ و بگوپال باشد درود

Mohl 4.624.3161–3

If the sky should turn in this way
and overshadow the love between two persons,

then in place of red wine let us have combat,
let us bring the bow and the lasso for ambush.

{117} We want the thunder of drums instead of a measure of a song,[30]
with swords and with iron maces let us salute.

The time for words is now running out:

چنین پاسخ آوردش اسفندیار   که گفتار چندین نیاید بکار

Mohl 4.626.3176

Esfandiyār thus answered him,
saying: "The time for talking has passed."

There is a desire to linger over the remaining moments of cheer at a feast that will soon come to an end:

بشوتن چنین گفت با میگسار   که بی آب یک جام دیگر بیار
می آورد و رامشگرانرا بخواند   ز رستم همی در شگفتی بماند

Mohl 4.626.3189–90

Beshutan[31] said thus to the wine steward:
"Bring another goblet not mixed with water."

He brought the wine and Beshutan called for the singers,
and he kept on marvelling at Rostam.

29. On programmatic descriptions of feasts as the context of good cheer *because* they are the context for the performance of epic, see Davidson 2013a[1994]:146–148.
30. That is, the context of their feasting together had been a context of song.
31. This character is acting here as Esfandiyār's master of ceremonies.

{118} Ironically, it is Esfandiyār, the one who is destined to lose the competition with Rostam and thus forfeit his life, who insists on bringing the feast to an end:

تو فردا ببینی ز مردان هنر   چو من تاختنرا ببندم کمر
تن خویش را نیز مستای هیچ   بایوان شو و کار فردا بسیچ
ببینی که من در صف کارزار   چنانم که با باده و میگسار

Mohl 4.628.3202–4

Tomorrow you will see how the brave show their prowess
when I gird myself to attack.

Do not praise your own strength.
Go to your palace and prepare yourself for tomorrow.

You will see I am the same way in the battle line
as I am when I am with wine and drinkers of wine.

Rostam feels empathy for Esfandiyār, but he must press on. He cannot afford to risk the poetics of blame, which would surely endanger his identity as an epic hero:

هم از بند او بد شود نام من   بد آید گشتاسپ فرجام من
بگرد جهان هر که راند سخن   نکوهیدن من نگردد کهن
که رستم ز دست جوانی نرست   بزابل شد و پای او را ببست {119}
همه نام من باز گردد بننگ   نماند زمن در جهان بوی و رنگ

Mohl 4.628.3212–5

Also, because of his [= Esfandiyār's] bonds my name would fall into disgrace,
and my end would come to ill because of Goshtāsp.

Throughout the world, wherever people tell tales,
the blaming of me would not grow old:

that Rostam did not escape from the hand of a young man,
who came to Zābol and bound his feet.

My name would become a continuous disgrace [*nang*];
neither fragrance nor color would remain of me in the world.

It is imperative for Rostam to maintain his epic reputation, as mediated in the 'assemblies'. With his reference to 'assemblies', Rostam's word alludes to the general audience that epic designates as its primary context:[32]

ولیکن همین خوب گفتار من   از این پس بگویند بر انجمن

Mohl 4.630.3221

However, just as I say good words about myself,
after this they will say good things about me in the assembly.

{120} What Rostam boasts about himself at a feast is presented as the germ of what epic performers will sing about him in 'assemblies'. In this way, epic narrative performance presents itself as the extension of the hero's own performance when he boasts about himself. That is, epic implicitly derives itself from the speech-act of the heroic boast.

It is time for Rostam, the hero as performer, to become the executor of the deeds for which he deserves to have his deeds performed in song. He issues his final challenge to Esfandiyār:

پگاه آی ودر جنگ چاره مساز   مکن زین سپس کار بر ما دراز
تو فردا ببینی باَوردگاه   که گیتی شود پیش چشمت سیاه
بدانی که پیکار مردان مرد   چگونه بود روز ننگ و نبرد

Mohl 4.632.3256–8

Come at dawn and do not be cunning in battle.
Do not extend your dealings with us after this.

Tomorrow you will see upon the battlefield
that the world will go black before your very eyes.

You will know how that battle is between manly men
on the day of shame [*nang*] and battle.

The hero-prince Esfandiyār is to learn the ultimate lesson, Rostam warns him:

که تا نیز با نامداران مرد   باَوردگه بر نجویی نبرد {121}

Mohl 4.632.3264

That again with a renowned man on the battlefield
you will never seek to do battle again.

32. On the convention of designating, in epic, the "assembly" as the most general audience of epic, see Davidson 2013a[1994]:21, 33.

The conclusion is straightforward: the words chosen in the epic tradition to express the verbal combat between Rostam and Esfandiyār are not just poetic words: they are the performance of a verbal duel framed within the performance of the epic *Shāhnāma.*[33]

33. For the argument that Ferdowsi's *Shāhnāma* was composed for performance and even as performance (and that the composition made the notion of "performance" homologous with the notion of "writing a book"), see again Essay Three.

Essay Seven

Women's Lamentations as Protest in the *Shāhnāma*[1]

{123} The thesis of this essay is that the "quotation" in Persian epic of a woman's laments matches "real-life" women's laments described by anthropologists who observe this genre as a living tradition.

The social institutions of lament can be defined as the expression—by singing—of grief over the death of someone, or over other such misfortunes. There are many different forms of lament in many different societies, but there is one salient characteristic shared by most of them: lament tends to be gender-specific, so that only women sing laments in some societies, while in others they sing laments that are distinct in form or style from those of men.[2] It is difficult to trace the traditions of women's lament in the written evidence of the medieval Islamic world, especially since the Prophet is quoted as having singled out "lamenting the dead" (*al-niyāḥa ʿalā ʾl-mayyit*) as one of the three pre-Islamic customs that had to be abandoned by Muslims (the other two being "invoking the planets to get rain" and "attacking genealogies").[3] Still, there is clear evidence from medieval Iran, in the form of "quoted" laments within the *Shāhnāma*. This essay will concentrate on one such lament, uttered by Tahmina {124} on the occasion of the killing of her son Sohrāb by Rostam.[4]

It may be objected that such a lament is a mere representation of a lament, not a "real" one: after all, a character inside an epic poem is uttering it. How can we trust the words that a poet puts into the mouth of a character from the remote heroic past of Iran? And yet, I will argue that both the form and the content of what Tahmina is quoted as saying corresponds closely

1. This essay is an expansion and development of Davidson 1998c.

2. See Rosenblatt, Walsh, and Jackson 1976.

3. For treatments of this expression see Fahd 1995 and Abdesselem 1977, especially pp. 97–104.

4. I follow in general the readings found in Mohl 1838–1878:2.188–192.1200–1460. The more "scientific" later editions of the *Shāhnāma* omit, on the basis of editorial assumptions with which I do not agree (see in general Essay Two of the present book), a number of verses included by Mohl. See Bertels *et al.* 1960–1971:2.258–261 and Khaleghi-Motlagh 1988–2008:2.198–199.1–35 (the relevant text is relegated to the *apparatus criticus* on those pages).

to what is found in "real" women's laments observed by ethnographers in a wide variety of societies where traditional customs like lamentation have survived to this day. A distinctive feature of such real women's laments is the element of gender-specific *protest*—against one's misfortune in particular *as a woman* and against one's destiny in general *as a woman*.[5]

To express an emotion like grief by way of song does not make it any less of an emotion, if we accept the anthropological argument that emotion is culturally constructed.[6] It can even be shown, on the basis of ethnographic observation, that a given lament's combination of singing and grieving can expand and enhance the actual experience of grief.[7] Thus the performance of a lament is a {125} matter of poetics, and I will argue that the poetics of Persian epic *require* the poet to observe the internal poetics of the laments that he represents. When Tahmina expresses her grief and anger over the death of her son Sohrāb at the hands of his own father Rostam, the words that epic chooses to express her expression are not just poetic words: they are the performance of a lament framed within the performance of the epic *Shāhnāma*.[8] The poetics of protest inherent in Tahmina's lament are thus "safely" framed within the overall poetics of kingly and heroic legitimation inherent in the overarching narrative of Ferdowsi's *Book of Kings*.[9]

For a close analogy, we may compare the framing of women's laments in the ancient Greek epic tradition, as in the Homeric *Iliad* as analyzed by Richard P. Martin.[10] For the study of oral poetics in general, Martin suggests that "we abandon the notion of 'genre' as a literary term and train ourselves in the anthropologist's working methods."[11] As Martin argues, the outer narrative of the *Iliad*, "quoting" the embedded speeches of characters in the narrative, is really representing the performance of oral genres. Such "embedded genres," as we have already noted in Essay Six, include lament, prayer, supplication, commanding, praising, insulting, and narrating from memory.

{126} Martin has demonstrated "the usefulness of considering every

5. For ethnographic studies of women's lament traditions in "tribal" societies of the Islamic world today, see, for example, Abu-Lughod 1985; see also Abu-Lughod 1999[1986], especially pp. 197–204. Another important work is Grima 1992.

6. Lutz 1986.

7. Feld 1990.

8. For the argument that Ferdowsi's *Shāhnāma* was composed *for* performance and even *as* performance (and that the composition made the notion of "performance" homologous with the notion of "writing a book"), see again Essay Three.

9. On undercurrents of political destabilization within the overall framework of the *Shāhnāma*, see Davis 1992.

10. Martin 1989.

11. Martin 1989:44.

speech within the poem [the *Iliad*] a composition in its own right, a poem within epic, subject to conventions of discourse."[12] Thus the "quoted" speeches of characters in the *Iliad* "are in fact stylized versions of pre-existing, already stylized verbal art forms such as lamenting, rebuking, boasting;" in short, "the *Iliad* itself consists of various 'genres' within epic."[13]

The oral poet can "recollect the way contemporary men and women speak," since "the diction of such embedded genres is most likely inherited and traditional; the rhetoric, on the other hand, is the locus of spontaneous composition in performance."[14] When we consider "the way in which the heroes speak to one another" we discover that they are "performing to fit the audience."[15] For example, the *Iliad* shows both Helen and Hekabe as "actually enacting laments," and they are "fulfilling an expected performance role, using a recognized genre ... to create dramatic effect."[16] But the dramatic effect of the framed performance can be achieved only if the drama of the framing narrative is a performance in its own right: "any tale in oral tradition ... makes sense only in performance."[17]

{127} For Tahmina's lament in the *Shāhnāma* to "make sense" as a woman's protest, it has to have both an interior intent, as a speech-act of and by itself, and an exterior intent, as a component of the larger speech-act that is the whole performance/composition of the *Book of Kings*.[18] In order to attempt a reconstruction of the interior intent, we must first look for various kinds of protest rhetoric as we find it attested in the real laments of real women in living traditions described by ethnographers.

In the case of living traditions of lament in Iranian societies, there is a wide variety of surviving evidence. Although the existing research on this evidence is limited, the results are most revealing. In this presentation, I highlight three relevant publications of research centering on Iranian traditions of lament, particularly women's lament:[19]

12. Martin 1989:197.

13. Martin 1989:225.

14. Martin 1989:85. For an application of Martin's methods to the surviving Arab oral epic traditions, in particular to the *Sīrat Banī Hilāl* epic, see again Reynolds 1995:207, already cited in Essay Six.

15. Martin 1989:85.

16. Martin 1989:87.

17. Martin 1989:129; as with "real" genres, there can be conflation: for example, "praise and lament are intertwined" (p. 144).

18. For anthropological applications of the concept of "speech act," see also Essay Six.

19. The Lori laments published in Vahman and Asatrian 1995 (pp. 69–81, 138–157) also correspond in various respects to the other Iranian traditions of lamentation that I discuss in this essay.

1. The research of Charles M. Kieffer on traditional laments performed by women in Dari-speaking communities around the area of Kābul in Afghanistan.[20] Kieffer also gives a most valuable bibliography on references to women's lament in ethnographic accounts dating from the twentieth and even the nineteenth century.[21]
2. The research of Benedicte Grima on traditional laments performed by women in Paxtun communities extending from Eastern Afghanistan to Pakistan's North West Frontier Province (especially the villages of Madyan and Ahmadi Banda).[22]
3. The research of Mohammad Mokri on traditional laments performed by professional women singers in Kurdish dialectal communities (especially in the Gurani dialect, in the Northern regions of the modern states of Iran and Iraq).[23]

As we can see from the research of Kieffer, women who perform lament are "exteriorizing" their emotions.[24] There are conventional poses for the singing: for example, a group of lamenting women will hold each other by the elbow[25] and will mix their singing with stylized sobs that prolong the words of lament, such as *bačé-éééém u-hu-hu-hu-hu* (or *i-hi-hi-hi-hi*).[26] There are different formulas that are most appropriate for grieving over different categories of loved ones who died, such as a son, a daughter, a father, a husband;[27] and there are important sub-categories, such as an infant son or a married son with children.[28]

The research of Grima extends the perspective on exteriorized emotions from the actual performance of lament to other forms of speech act involving not only the emotion of *gham* 'sorrow' but even the emotion of *xādi* 'joy'. She makes it clear, however, that the primary emotion in the wide spectrum of speech acts traditionally performed by Paxtun women is still *gham*, and that the primary sorrow is over instances of death. Particularly well documented are instances of lament over the deaths of sons.[29] Two specific words

20. Kieffer 1975.
21. Kieffer 1975:322n36.
22. Grima 1992.
23. Mokri 1995.
24. Kieffer 1975:313.
25. Kieffer 1975:315.
26. Kieffer 1975:316.
27. Kieffer 1975:316–318.
28. Kieffer 1975:317.
29. Grima 1992:59.

that refer to such lament are *sānda*, which can best be translated as 'lament',[30] and *zharā* or 'weeping'.[31] As Grima makes clear, the *gham* 'sorrow' expressed by women's lament has the effect of a "structured resistance" to the sufferings endured by women within the context of Paxtun society, and that this "resistance" is perceived by men as a potential threat to their own identity.[32] This model of Paxtun women's "structured resistance," as developed by Grima, is relevant to the model of "protest" as I have developed it here.

As for the research of Mokri, it is confined mostly to the laments performed by professional female performers in the Gurani dialect of Kurdish. From the evidence collected by this researcher, it is clear that professionalism in the performance of lament is secondary to the non-professional lamentations of women who mourn their own loved ones.

It is also clear, as Mokri points out in passing, that the Iranian Shiᶜite traditions of lament for the two Imams are another secondary development, as reflected by the specialized word *nawḥa-gar*.[33] There is no space here in this presentation for me to delve into the highly complex history of Shiᶜite traditions of lamentation, and I must stay on track here by focusing on the main interest of Mokri, which is most relevant to the lament of Tahmina as quoted in the *Shāhnāma*.

In the case of Kurdish women's traditional laments, a most characteristic theme is the sorrow expressed by the main characters in the story of Khosrow and Shirin. In other words, this sorrowful story is the inspiration, as it were, for the laments performed by women to express their own sorrow over the deaths of their own loved ones, or, in the case of professional female mourners, over the deaths of others. The Kurdish female mourners actually identify their own sorrow with the sorrow inherent in the story of Khosrow and Shirin, which in turn is expressed by many different versions of laments sung by the character of the beautiful queen Shirin herself over the deaths of the two male love interests in the story, Farhād the charismatic artisan and Khosrow himself, the queen's husband. There are also many different versions of laments sung by Farhād over the false news of the death of Shirin. Such laments by Shirin and Farhād are lavishly quoted, as it were, in Kurdish oral traditions of women's lament as studied by Mokri. And, in one case, the lament of Farhād over the false news of the death of Shirin is actually quoted in the classical version of the story as composed by the great poet Neẓāmi in the twelfth century. In the *Khosrow and Shirin* of Neẓāmi, the

30. Grima 1992:59.
31. Grima 1992:59.
32. Grima 1992:140, 147.
33. Mokri 1995:464.

lament of Farhād over Shirin is embedded in the poet's poetry, as if it were a direct quotation. And there is a wealth of further quotations of further laments by Shirin and Farhād in the body of classicizing Kurdish poetry as documented by Mokri.

Besides the Iranian evidence that we have considered so far, we may also compare non-Iranian evidence. To engage in this kind of comparison is useful for achieving insights that are valid from the standpoint of comparative sociology. Whatever points of comparison we discover can be described as *typological parallels*—and here I am using a term that is most familiar in descriptive linguistics.

Among the typological parallels that are available for study, perhaps the most useful is the evidence of Modern Greek lament traditions as studied by such anthropologists as Loring Danforth,[34] Anna Caraveli,[35] Nadia Seremetakis,[36] and Michael Herzfeld.[37] There are also important contributions by Classicists and literary critics, most notably those of Margaret Alexiou[38] and Gail Holst-Warhaft.[39]

It is in fact from the title of Caraveli's work that I derive the word "protest" in the title of my essay here. Her study "has proved particularly effective in showing how laments may permit the subversion of authoritative orders, not through direct, frontal rhetoric but through challenges to normative articulacy."[40] As for Seremetakis, {128} she argues that women's performance of ritual lament "publicly resists those male-dominated institutions and discourses that fragment the female practice and devalue the social status of women's labor."[41] By implication, such "resistance" would express discontent not only with the lamenter's here-and-now but also with male-centered traditions in general.

Still, as Herzfeld cautions, there are limits to the pursuit of this line of thinking: "A search for 'the' meaning of these texts ... hardly improves on survivalist and nationalist dreams of finding 'the' origins, or on teleological analyses of 'the' functions, of such phenomena."[42] He goes on to ask the basic

34. Danforth 1982:169–194.

35. Caraveli 1986.

36. Seremetakis 1990.

37. Herzfeld 1993.

38. Alexiou 2002[1974]. For me this book remains the basic study of the subject of the continuities and discontinuities of women's lament traditions in Greek society—all the way from ancient times to the present.

39. Holst-Warhaft 1992.

40. Herzfeld 1993:243.

41. Seremetakis 1990:507.

42. Herzfeld 1993:242.

question: do laments really change anything?[43] Referring to one particular lament that he collected in Crete as the "key text" for his interpretation, Herzfeld shows how this song, performed by a young woman mourning the death of her elderly husband, "bewails loss and destruction [here he has just given us a minimalist definition of lament], ... but may also have initiated a process that allowed a young woman to redress her low social status."[44] Herzfeld's point is that the words of the given young woman who is recorded in his case study as lamenting the death of her husband cannot be understood without taking into consideration not only the short-term but even the long-term effects that her lament had produced for the community that had heard her.

{129} Herzfeld stresses the "indeterminacy" of performance, which helps explain "... why some events seem significant in hindsight even when at the time they may not have seemed significant at all."[45] In other words, performance creates meaning for the composition.

The lamenting woman whom Herzfeld recorded "did not resign herself to what others regarded as her 'fate' but rather, through her lament and subsequent actions, she took control over her 'fate'."[46] In Modern Greek, in fact, the word for 'lament' is *mirolóyi*, meaning 'words about fate'.[47]

The idea of "managing fate," Herzfeld argues, is a paradox only if we take "fate" at face value. Herzfeld explains it this way: when society blames the grieving person for his or her misfortune, with the attitude that it must have been brought on because of some moral flaw, then the grieving person can say that the misfortune was fated to be and there was nothing that could be done to prevent it: "The logic of fate and personality is clear: my failures and your successes are just a matter of luck, whereas my successes and your failures are proof of radical differences in 'character'."[48] The inherent ambiguity, Herzfeld concludes, leaves open the possibility of future action.

Paradoxically, then, the more the lamenter blames fate and her inability to control fate, the more she takes her own fate into her own hands—in the eyes of those who hear her lament. Further, the {130} more she involves others in her grief, the more power she has to protest her own fate. In order to achieve the fullest possible range of grief, the lamenter must make the view of her grief as public as possible. For example, in Modern Greek traditions a

43. Herzfeld 1993:242.

44. Herzfeld 1993:242. When he says "the text" in this context, he means simply the text of the recording of the young woman's *performance* of the lament.

45. Herzfeld 1993:242.

46. Herzfeld 1993:242.

47. Nagy 1999a[1979]:80n23.

48. Herzfeld 1993:242.

mother who has lost her son can most effectively achieve "the public view of personal disaster" by linking the passion of Christ with the death of her son: if a lamenting person can "evoke a sufficiently rich image of collective suffering, she will move others to tears because she has recast individual as common experience, her personal pain as a shared past and present."[49]

We have seen the same kind of linking in the Kurdish traditions of women's lament, where the sorrows of larger-than-life figures like Shirin and Farhād are the fuel for expressing the sorrows of real women in performing their own lamentations over the deaths of their loved ones.

With these points of comparison in mind, let us proceed to a close reading of the passage from the *Shāhnāma* "quoting" the lament of Tahmina. She mourns the death of her son, Sohrāb, who has just been killed in battle by his own father, Rostam. The following is a brief outline of the events that lead up to this tragic end:

> Rostam goes on a hunting expedition completely alone (with the exception of his horse, Rakhsh) outside of Iran, into the Turanian wildland. After a large, solitary meal, he falls asleep, having let Rakhsh roam free without his bridle. Some Turkomans, seeing that Rostam is off his guard, use this opportunity to steal Rakhsh. When Rostam wakes up and finds that Rakhsh has disappeared, he is devastated. He goes to the city Samangān, to find his horse and is invited by the King to stay with a promise of help. The king's daughter, Tahmina, comes to him in the middle of the night and tells him that if he were to impregnate her she would get him back his horse. Rostam accepts her proposition and then, the next day, when they part, he gives her an armband with the instructions that, should she bear a son, she is to put this armband on the child so that his father could {131} recognize him. A son is born and is named Sohrāb. He shares the same early characteristics that his father had, looking a year old when he is only a month old, using weapons when he is only three, and other such traits that distinguish him as a hero. When he learns from his mother who his father is, he leaves Turan, with a Turanian army of warriors, to find Rostam. He sets out on his search for his father with the intention that once he has found Rostam, the two of them could then overthrow the Shāh, Key Kāʾus, and put Rostam on the Iranian throne. Then they would overthrow the ruler of Turan, Afrāsiyāb, and put Sohrāb on the Turanian throne. Father and son would then rule the world, in a manner of speaking, being such a powerful, combined force. Consequently, as he sets out to find his father he also sets out to invade Iran.

49. Herzfeld 1993:242.

> Afrāsiyāb, the king of Turan and enemy of Iran, is willing to have Sohrāb invade Iran because he hopes that, once pitted against his father, Sohrāb would overcome him, thereby leaving Iran completely defenseless, if it lost its 'world hero' *pahlavān-e jahān*.[50] He plots that even if Rostam should kill Sohrāb, instead of the other way around, the guilt of filicide would consume him for the rest of his days. In this scheme, Sohrāb must never recognize his father or else he will not fight him.
>
> As Sohrāb invades Iran, he wreaks havoc on the outskirts, fighting the "amazon," Gordafrid, and wasting her territory. The Iranian throne panics and summons Rostam to help in this state of emergency. Rostam does not take any threat from Turan seriously, and he does not immediately obey the Shāh's command, but feasts drunkenly for three days instead. When he finally does come as summoned, the Shāh, because of his delay, is furious with him and publicly dishonors him. Rostam withdraws in anger but, fearful of being accused of cowardice, he eventually agrees to fight Sohrāb, not knowing, however, that Sohrāb is his own son. Before the two {132} meet for a one-on-one confrontation, Sohrāb terrorizes the Iranian host, forcing it to scatter and causing chaos. Rostam and Sohrab then fight, first with weapons, then by wrestling, but draw apart when evening comes. On the second day, Sohrāb overpowers Rostam in a wrestling match and is about to finish him off when Rostam tricks him by telling him that it is Iranian tradition that one has to defeat the opponent twice before one can take his head. Sohrāb accepts this lie and runs off after an antelope. Rostam meanwhile, exhausted, asks *khodā* or 'God' to give him back his former strength, for he used to have such density that his feet would sink into rocks. Finally, on the third day, having tricked Sohrāb out of his victory, Rostam kills Sohrāb, only to learn afterwards the sad truth about his identity. Overcome with grief, he asks Key Kāʾus to restore his son's life, but Key Kāʾus refuses on grounds that two such outstanding champions might be a threat to the throne.

What follows is my translation of Tahmina's lament, segmented here into series of stages, with commentary attached to each stage:[51]

همی گفت که ای جان مادر کنون   کجایی سرشته بخاک اندرون
چو چشمم بره بود گفتم مگر   بیابم ز فرزند و رستم خبر

50. More on this theme in Davidson 2013a[1994]:114–125.

51. I am using the term "stage" in light of the model "five stages of death" introduced by Elisabeth Kubler-Ross 1969.

گمانم چنان بود گفتم کنون   بگشتی بگرد جهان اندرون
پدررا همی جستی و یافتی   کنون بآمدن تیز بشتافتی

Mohl 2.188.1407–10

> {133} She said all at once: 'O soul of your mother
> Where are you now? Mingled with the dust?
>
> When my eyes were fixed on the road I said
> "Perhaps I will learn news of my child and Rostam."
>
> My *gomān* ["fancy" or "suspicion"] was thus, and I said, "now you are wandering around the world,
>
> searching continuously, and now, having found your father, you now hasten to return."'

Tahmina both denies and accepts the death of her son. This ambiguity between angry denial and abject resignation corresponds to an ambiguous self-characterization. She speaks with the voice of a woman of all ages of life, be it a young bride who has just become the mother of a first-born or be it a bitter old widow who has known all along the cruelty of a world where men are fated to wage war. The universalized image of a grieving woman enhances the rhetoric of "the public view of personal disaster."

Tahmina simultaneously plays two roles: she is trusting, but dumbfounded, a mother who cannot believe what has happened—and yet has suspected the truth all along. In denial, she addresses her lament to her son as if he were alive. She begins by asking him where he is. She then tells him that she has anxiously been waiting for him, expecting at least to hear about him. She depicts herself as any mother who is expecting her child's return home, reassuring herself that she will soon learn of his whereabouts. She then says that it was her *gomān*, which can be interpreted positively as 'imagination' or 'fancy' and negatively as 'suspicion,' that Sohrāb, {134} having departed in search of his father, is now hastening homewards. She is both imagining his coming home so that they may have a joyful reunion and recognizing that such a reunion is going to be only in her imagination, never in reality. Joyful expectation and the sad shattering of that expectation combine as one feeling.

Tahmina is like a sentinel, looking out to see what is coming down the road, picturing herself as expecting something that will never happen: the sight of her son coming home with his father, her husband. This image, of course, matches her vision of her son, who is in turn pictured as a sentinel, on the lookout, seeking his father throughout the world. This double sentinel duty of mother and son, with her staying ever on the lookout, with her eyes fixed on the road, while he keeps scanning the world, looking for his father, underscores the interplay of naive expectations and harsh reality—and yet it turns reality into expectation, upside down, inside out. If it is just her imagination that Sohrāb is looking out for his father, then the reality is that not only did he search for his father but he found him. Yet what she so confidently says she expects, news about Sohrāb and Rostam, perhaps even seeing the two of them coming home to her together, is a shattered hope. The shift of her 'fancy' back to the reality of what is at hand sets the audience up for the next stage of her lament:

چو دانستم ای پور که آید خبر   که رستم دریدن بخنجر جگر

Mohl 2.188.1411

'How could I know, O son, when the news came
that Rostam would pierce your liver with a dagger?'

{135} She now gets straight to the point, mincing no words. This is not only the last thing she expected, but she sees no reason why she should have expected it in the first place. The abrupt switch—from her almost disbelieving that Sohrāb is really dead and her not even mentioning his father's hand in the son's death—to her furious and irrefutable statement of fact is cloaked in a rhetorical question. She speaks in the voice not only of any woman of any age but of any man. What man, in his right mind, would deliberately kill his own child? Surely such a man is not human:

دریغش نیآمد بر آن روی تو   بر آن برز بالا و آن موی تو
بر آن گردگاهش نیآمد دریغ   که بدرید رستم مر آن را بتیغ

Mohl 2.188.1412–3

'Didn't he have regrets, sorrow or pity [*darigh*],
when he saw your face, your tall stature and hair?

Had he no pity upon your middle [*gerdgāh*]—that very thing
which Rostam lacerated with his sword?'

As Tahmina continues to express her misery at this outrage, she plays up the difference between her humanity and Rostam's lack of it by pointing out how the father failed to recognize in his son what she as a mother knew so intimately. Tahmina expresses such pride as she describes her son, whom she reared into early manhood, with the intimate detail of his hair, something that would not be seen by all, especially in battle, since Sohrāb would then be wearing {136} a helmet. By mentioning his hair and then moving on to his *gerdgāh*, which not only means 'middle' but also 'navel,' she emphasizes her own attachment to Sohrāb, because only *she* as a mother, and she alone, was once physically connected to Sohrāb, as she nourished him *in utero*. There is a striking parallel in Kurdish women's laments, where the interjection *rō/rū* is used frequently in the sense of 'alas!': this interjection is actually derived from the word *rūd* or *rūda*, meaning 'umbilical cord'.[52] The lament of Tahmina now turns to the audience, asking them how they could expect such a savage man as Rostam to act otherwise. Rostam had only seen Sohrāb once in his life and that was in battle. She furthers her case with the image of Rostam tearing out Sohrāb's *gerdgāh*. By ripping apart where the umbilical cord of Sohrāb once had been, that very means through which the mother had nourished the child when he was in her womb, the father Rostam has shown himself to be as viciously non-nurturing as the mother Tahmina is nurturing. He is the antithesis of what she is. She is Sohrāb's generator, Rostam is his destroyer:

بپرورده بودم تنت را بناز　　ببر بر بروز و شبان دراز
کنون آن بخون اندرون غرقه گشت　　کفن بربر و یال تو خرقه گشت
کنون من کرا گیرم اندر کنار　　که باشد همی مرمرا غمگسار
کرا خوانم اکنون بجای توپیش　　کرا گویم این درد و تیمار خویش

Mohl 2.188–90.1414–7

'I had nursed your body with tenderness
holding you to my breast during the long days and nights.

Now it is drowning in blood—
a shroud has become the tattered garment covering your breast and shoulder.

Whom can I now draw to my side?
{137} Who will forever be my confidant [*ghamgosār*]?

Whom can I summon in your place?
To whom can I tell my personal pain and sorrow?'

Tahmina now shifts the attention away from Rostam and back to Sohrāb as she once again addresses him directly. She recollects her role as a young mother, cherishing the body OF her nursling, and then bitterly declares it

52. Mokri 1995:465–466.

was all for nothing. She also contrasts her protective and continuous caring for her child with his present defenseless and sunken condition. Although Rostam is to blame for Sohrāb's destruction, Tahmina now blames her own son, not her husband. By dying, Sohrāb has abandoned her.[53] He has squandered her care. Now she is alone and has nobody. As she accuses Sohrāb of abandoning her when she asks him whom can she hold in her arms, who will be her *ghamgosār*, or confidant, who will sit next to her, and to whom will she tell about her pain and her sorrow, she is also blaming her son Sohrāb for not bringing her husband Rostam back to her to fulfill his role *as a husband*. Rostam should be the one to fulfill the role of a confidant to Tahmina—someone to fill her aching, lonely arms. She addresses her son as if he were her lover who had abandoned her. He was everything to her and she had given her life to him. How *dare* he leave her?

دریغاتن و جان و چشم و چراغ   بخاک‌اندرون‌مانده‌ازکاخ‌وباغ {138}
پدر جستی ای شیر لشکر پناه   بجای پدر گورت آمد براه
از امید نومید گشتی براز   بخفتی بخاک اندرون زاروار

Mohl 2.190.1418–20

'Alas for his body and soul, eyes and light
all stay in the dust, away from the palace and garden.

You searched for your father, O Lion, O Army Protector
in place of your father, you came upon your tomb.

With affliction you pass from hope to despair;
miserably you sleep upon the ground.'

As she bewails his body, the very body that she had nurtured and that Rostam had failed to appreciate, she also bewails that her son's body now lies in the dust, not in the splendor to which it is entitled. The timbre is more general, and can apply to any young man, cut down in his prime, thereby inviting the audience to think beyond Sohrāb and about others in a similar plight. The awful truth peculiar to this story, that Sohrāb did actually find what he was looking for (his father)—and look what it got him (a dagger in the liver from his own father's hand)—is reshaped to look like a failed quest that ended with the hero's death. Her addressing him as a mighty warrior who found his death instead of his quest makes her personal loss everyone's

53. On the typology of the lamenter's conventional blaming of the beloved dead for his abandoning her and leaving her reputation and her very safety vulnerable, see Holst-Warhaft 1992:112.

loss. The son has turned from hope to hopeless despair (*zār* meaning lamentation as well) since he is sleeping in the dust, enveloped by a lamentable condition (*zārwār*). So too the audience is now completely enveloped by despair and grief:

از آن پیش کودشنه را بر کشید   جگرگاه سیمین تو بر درید {139}
چرا آن نشانی که مادرت داد   ندادی بدو و نکریش یاد
نشان داده بود از پدر مادرت   ز بهر چه نآمد همی باورت
کنون مادرت ماند بی تو اسیر   پر از رنج و تیمار و درد و زخیر
چرا بآمدم با تو اندر سفر   که گشتی بکام دلت ماه و خور
مرا رستم از دور بشناختی   ترا با من ای پور بنواختی
نینداختی نیزه نزدت فراز   نکردی جگرگاه ای پور باز

Mohl 2.190.1421–7

> 'Before, when he drew forth his dagger
> and sliced your silvery abdomen
>
> why did you not show him that sign which your mother had given you?
> Why didn't you make him mindful.
>
> Your mother had given you a sign from your father.
> Why did you not believe her?
>
> Now your mother will remain a prisoner without you,
> full of suffering and grief, pain and aches in the belly.
>
> Why didn't I fare along with you
> when you turned your heart's desire, the moon and the sun.
>
> Rostam would have recognized me from afar,
> (if you were) with me, O Son, he would have treated you humanely.
>
> {140} He would not have pitched a javelin at you,
> he would not have demolished your bowels, O my son.'

She concludes her lament by shifting inward again, away from public sympathy and away from public outrage to scolding her son for not doing as she had advised. She blames him for his death and blames him further for causing her such misery. Her temper is that of a mother scolding a child for being disobedient and then pointing out the consequences of his irresponsible behavior. Now his death is his own fault because he could have prevented it if he had only listened to her. Finally, having blamed him, she blames herself. As any mother after the death of her child, she blames herself for not preventing it, even if there was nothing that she could have done about it. If only she had gone with him, then nothing would have happened to him. She fancies that Rostam would have recognized her from afar and embraced them both, instead of—and now she switches back to reality—what really happened, that Rostam stabbed Sohrāb, his very own son, in the liver.

After the epic finishes "quoting" her lament, it tells how Tahmina gathers up all of Sohrāb's possessions and armor, takes his sword and docks his horse's tail, and then distributes his possessions among the poor. In doing this, she, in effect, annihilates his accoutrements by transforming them into something else. Instead of leaving his armor for someone to inherit, along with the heroic identity that is passed on from its previous owner, she gives it away as alms to the poor. And by docking the steed's tail she has seemingly transformed Sohrāb's war horse into a cart horse. In other words she turns swords into ploughshares.

{141} These Acts of Tahmina, performed after the performance of her lament, reinforce the words of protest expressed by the lament itself. They make explicit the threat that women's lament implicitly poses to institutions that depend on the solidarity of men. Gail Holst-Warhaft describes this kind of threat in ancient as well as present-day Greek society:

> Once any state has need of a standing army, it must condemn the negative, bitter pain of traditional laments; otherwise how will it recruit volunteers and keep their loyalty? Similarly, once a state has established courts of law, how can it tolerate the cycle of revenge such as the one triggered by female lamenters at the tomb of Agamemnon, or the threat of anarchy posed by laments like that of the widow Vrettis from Mani in the Peloponnese, who, when her only son was killed by neighbours, pulled out her knife in the courtroom, bit it and said:
>
> Mr. President,
> if you do not condemn them
> to death of a life sentence—
> you see this dagger?
> I'll go to the upper quarter
> and if I can't find a grown-up
> I'll grab a small child
> and slay him like a lamb—
> for mine was an only child
> and they cut him to pieces.[54]

54. Holst-Warhaft 1992:5, quoting from Kassis 1979:74.

Such words are threatening not only because of what they say {142} but also, even more important, for what they are: a song of lament. The agenda of protest in a lament may be quite explicitly threatening, as here, or only implicitly so, as when a mother's grief over the loss of a child in a war demoralizes the host of fighting men.

In the case of Tahmina's lament, of course, the potential demoralization is far worse, since the death of the child reflects the brutality of the father, who is Rostam, the paragon of Iranian warriors. In this case, the mother's lament is a threat not only to the "army," the aggregate of Iranian warriors: it is also a threat to the heroic status of the warrior who is the paragon of the "army"—and even to the epic that glorifies that paragon, the *Shāhnāma* itself. The lament of Tahmina, contained by the epic, is an implicit threat to that epic. The fact that epic frames the lament, however, can attenuate the threat, since the framework can reassert male solidarity that is threatened by the female voice of lament. This reassertion is done by the "quoting" of a male warrior immediately after the "quoting" of Tahmina. The dramatic occasion for the speech of this male speaker, Bahmān, is the anniversary of Sohrāb's death. In this way, epic asserts the male voice after a "cooling off" period of one year. Although this heroic speech sustains some of the themes that pervade Tahmina's lament, it reworks these themes to accommodate the dominant agenda of the framing epic:

چنین گفت بهرام نیکوسخن   که با مردگان آشنایی مکن {143}
نه ایدر همی ماند خواهی دراز   بسیچیده باش و درنگی مساز
بتو داد یکروز نوبت پدر   سزدگر ترا نوبت آید بسر
چنینست رازش نیاَید پدید   نیابی بخیره چه جویی کلید
در بسته را کس نداند کشاد   درین رنج عمر تو گردد بباد
ولیکن که اندر گذشت از قضا   چنین بد قضا از خداوند ما
دل اندر سرای سپنجی مبند   سپنجی مباشد بسی سودمند

Mohl 2.192.1452–8[55]

Thus the eloquent Bahrām said
'Do not befriend the dead.

You will not stay here for a long time.
Be equipped and do not fashion delay.

On a day your father gave you the appointed time (*nowbat*),
is it right that this time comes to an end for you?

55. Bertels *et al.* 1960–1971:2.249–250; Khaleghi-Motlagh 1988–2008:2.199.

Thus his secret does not become manifest.
You will not find it in your bewilderment, so why do you seek the key?

No one knows how to open the firmly shut door.
In this anguished endeavor, your life will turn into the wind.

But however he fared, it was the judgment of fate;
thus is fate allotted to us by God.

Do not bind your heart to the ephemeral world.
The ephemeral is not sufficiently profitable.'

{144} It seems as if Tahmina's rhetoric in pretending that Sohrāb is not dead and still looking for his father is maintained by Bahrām's speech, but for different ends. Bahrām is in effect asking the restless spirit of the dead to stop looking for his father. In the upside-down and inside-out world created by Tahmina's lament, it is the realm of the dead, not of the real world, that is ephemeral. Since Sohrāb continues to be addressed as if he were still alive, the ephemeral world of the living can be reassigned to the world of the dead. In this way, the words of Bahrām can unthink the implicit threat of revenge from the restless spirit of the dead son of Rostam. The threat conjured up by Tahmina's words of lament can now be dissipated into the insubstantial shades of the dead.

Essay Eight

Observations on a Study of *naqqāli* Performances of Persian Epics

Kumiko Yamamoto's book *The Oral Background of Persian Epics* is based on a doctoral thesis submitted to the School of Oriental and African Studies, University of London, in 2000. It has to do with a Persian tradition known as the *naqqāli*, a form of storytelling performed by a professional storyteller or *naqqāl*. The tradition as we know it took shape in the Safavid period (1501–1736 CE) and is therefore linked with distinctly Shiʿite social settings. There are marginal survivals of the *naqqāli* performance tradition in present-day Iran, and the author notes that she has actually heard such a performance at a coffee house in Tehran.[1] The *naqqāli* performance that she heard is foundational for her book. The tradition underlying this performance by Morshed Vali-Allāh Torābi, whom she describes as the "*naqqāl* of the present book," turns out to have wide-ranging implications for the study of Persian oral traditions.

The book is volume 26 in the series "Brill Studies in Middle Eastern Literatures," edited by Susanne Pinckney Stetkevych, which is a reconfigured continuation of the earlier series "Studies in Arabic Literature." The formal description of the new series, as printed on the opening page to the left of the book's title page, announces that literatures other than the Arabic are now included ("Persian, Turkish, etc."). "As in the past," the description goes on to say, "the series aims to publish literary critical and historical studies on a broad range of literary materials: classical and modern, written and oral, poetry and prose." The wording reveals, however, that things are not exactly what they had been "in the past." To describe literary materials as "written and oral" is to recognize a reality that has often been neglected in the study of traditional literatures. And the reality is this: at least some literary traditions are grounded in oral traditions. The present book, *The Oral Background of Persian Epics*, is a work of literary scholarship that recognizes such a reality.

1. Yamamoto 2003:ix.

As the title indicates, the author (hereafter "Y.") seeks to show that the literary tradition of Persian "epics," as exemplified by the *Shāhnāma* of Ferdowsi (completed around 1000 CE) and the *Garshāspnāma* of Asadi (1064–66 CE), was grounded in an oral tradition; further, as the subtitle suggests, such an oral tradition in poetry was somehow related to an oral tradition of storytelling in prose known as the *naqqāli* tradition. I say "somehow" for the moment, since Y. does not commit herself regarding what the formal relationship might be between such oral traditions in poetry and prose.

The oral traditional nature of *naqqāli* performance has been studied before. An outstanding example is the pioneering research of Mary-Ellen Page, who has thoroughly analyzed the traditions of *naqqāli* performance and has linked these traditions with a form of text known in Persian as the *tumār*.[2] The *tumār* is a scroll used as an aide-mémoire by the *naqqāl*. It can be described as a long prompt-book or chap-book. In developing her relevant arguments, Y. relies heavily on Page's work on (1) *naqqāli* performance and (2) the relationship of such performance with the *tumār*. The importance of this earlier work of Page is evident from Y.'s occasional references to it.[3] Others as well have relied on Page's work in developing their own relevant arguments, myself included.[4]

Y. also relies on recent publications of *naqqāli* texts. Y.'s detailed analysis of a narrative found in one such text is the core of her book. The title of the narrative is *Dāstān-e Rostam va Sohrāb: Revāyat-e Naqqālān* 'The Story of Rostam and Sohrāb: The Storytellers' Narrative,' by Morshed ʿAbbās Zariri, which is part of a thousand-page *tumār* entitled *Zariri-nāma* 'The Book of Zariri'.[5]

The most explicit evidence about earlier attested phases of the *naqqāli* tradition comes from the Safavid period (1501–1736 CE). The founder of the Safavid dynasty, Shāh Esmāʿil I (ruled ca. 1501–24 CE), is known to have made use of *naqqāl* performers in promoting his Shiʿite régime. Different groupings of such performers were assigned to different sectors of the population, such as the military and members of the *zurkhāna*.[6]

In the Safavid period, the *naqqāli* tradition had still accommodated a wide range of "epics" and "romances," but the tradition declined in later periods, and its range was considerably narrowed.[7] Granted, there was some continuity. Even in the early twentieth century, "some 5,000 to 10,000 der-

2. Page 1977, 1979.

3. See for example Y. pp. xxiin20, 29n30.

4. Davidson 2013a[1994]:49–52. My argumentation about *naqqāli* performances and related texts is not mentioned by Y.

5. Dustxᵛāh 1990.

6. Documentation in Y. p. 21.

7. Y. p. 28.

vishes engaged in various forms of oral tradition, including *naqqāli*."[8] By the mid-1970s, however, as we learn from the data reported by Page, there were only four professional *naqqāli* storytellers still to be found in a place like Shiraz.

Given the obsolescence of the *naqqāli* tradition, we cannot be sure that we have a representative sample to work with. Still, what little has survived can be used as evidence for reconstructing earlier phases of this tradition. And the work of Y. in attempting such a reconstruction is the most important and valuable aspect of her research, which is based primarily on an analysis of a live *naqqāli* performance by the *naqqāl* Torābi, combined with an analysis of the narrative about Rostam and Sohrāb taken from the thousand-page *tumār* of Zariri.

A high point of the book is this description of a performance by Torābi:

> Upon arrival at a coffee house Torābi prepared what he called a *sardam* ('platform') by piling up tables and chairs on which he placed a *tumār*. About four o'clock in the afternoon he ordered his pupil to strike the gong which hung from the ceiling, handing over a stick to him. The pupil called for a *salavāt* prayer and recited verses which concluded with a *salavāt*. Once the stick was returned[,] Torābi, for his part, recited a *salavāt* and a few verses. He called for another *salavāt* before moving on to the day's session. He then proceeded to the centre of the coffee house and began telling a story in prose. Concentrating on telling, he frequently gesticulated with the stick (which sometimes represented a horse and sometimes a sword) and raised his voice. About half an hour later, he turned to the platform to say a prayer to [*sic*] Muhammad and to recite poetry. After repeating this once again, he struck the gong and called for a *salavāt*. He then picked up the story from where he had left off. About thirty minutes later, he exchanged a *salavāt* with his audience and went on to read verse passages. Once again he called for a *salavāt* and continued the story for about a quarter of an hour. Approximately fifteen minutes before the ending, he made a turn to collect money from members of the audience, all the while calling for prayers to [*sic*] the Prophet.[9]

Piecing together what she has learned from her own experience and from the earlier experiences of researchers like Page, Y. offers this summary:

> In *naqqāli* the stories were told in instalments, each lasting for about ninety minutes. Some storytellers gave two sessions a day (one in the morning and the other in the evening) and continued the same

8. Y. p. 22.
9. Y. pp. 24–25.

> story over six months. Others, like Torābi, gave one session a day and completed the *Shāhnāma* in about six months.[10]

In the case of Torābi, his *naqqāli* version of the *Shāhnāma* ended with the reign of Bahman. For this performer, the *naqqāli* repertoire was restricted to the "Book of Kings" tradition, but there is considerable evidence to show that the repertoires of earlier *naqqāli* performers were far broader in scope, including other "epics" and even "romances."[11]

In this connection, I agree with Y. that, despite claims to the contrary, the coffee house was a traditional venue for such *naqqāli* performances as far back as in Safavid times.[12]

I also agree that the interweaving of poetry with the prose of a *naqqāl* like Torābi is a traditional aspect of the *naqqāli* tradition, attested also in the texts of the *tumār*-s:

> When the storyteller told a prose story he stood at the centre of the coffee house; when reciting verses he installed himself at the platform or *sardam*. In terms of the narrative structure too, verses which appear intermittently in the *tumār* text are used, for example, to enhance dramatic effects, to express the internal feelings of characters, or to sum up the story.[13]

I should add that similar patterns in the interweaving of poetry with prose are attested in a wide variety of oral traditions.[14]

Y. speaks of *naqqāli* performances in terms of performance units or "sessions," which she terms "instalments"[15] (from here on, I will use the spelling "installment"). We see here a most valuable aspect of Y.'s argumentation. The overall narrative of the *naqqāl* is divided into smaller narrative units that are conditioned by the framework of performance units or installments. These installments have an average duration of ninety minutes. By way of *installment divisions*, the overall narrative becomes *serialized*.

Serialization, from one installment to the next, is a special way of composing or even recomposing an overall narrative in terms of smaller narrative units constrained by limitations in time. Each installment is complete short-range but incomplete long-range, and the tension between completeness and incompleteness enhances the narrative artistry, producing effects of suspense and even surprise in the construction of the plot.

10. Y. p. 24.
11. Y. p. 28.
12. Y. p. 28n47; also p. 21.
13. Y. p. 28.
14. There is a relevant discussion by Davidson 2013a[1994]:51, not cited by Y.
15. Y. p. 24.

I should add that the phenomenon of composing or recomposing an overall narrative by serializing it in smaller narrative units constrained by limitations in time is attested in other performance traditions as well: a case in point is the principle of *equalized weighting* in ancient Greek traditions of rhapsodic performance.[16]

Y. goes on to test what she has learned about installment divisions in live *naqqāli* performance by attempting to reconstruct corresponding installment divisions in the text of the *tumār* of Zariri. Then she goes even further by attempting similar reconstructions in sample texts of the *Shāhnāma* of Ferdowsi and the *Garshāspnāma* of Asadi. In the context of these reconstructions, she offers an illuminating analysis of narrative markers, which she tries to distinguish—unnecessarily, in my opinion—from what she calls "temporal markers." A high point of this analysis is her description of "markers of contingency," indicating "the improvement or worsening of a character's state."[17]

These reconstructions, in the form of three appendices at the end,[18] fill up a great deal of space for a book as short as this one. The titles for Appendices 1, 2, and 3 all start with the phrase "The Hypothetical Instalment Divisions," corresponding to (1) the selected narrative from the *tumār* of Zariri, (2) "Story 13B" in the *Shāhnāma*, and (3) the story of the battle between Garshāsp and Bahu in the *Garshāspnāma*.

The question is, are these reconstructions really useful? I raise the question because, despite Y.'s awareness that her installment divisions are "hypothetical," she all too often slips into a mode of speaking that makes it seem as if her hypotheses are facts. For example, there is a table entitled "Epics in *Naqqāli*,"[19] where the first entry to be listed is the *Shāhnāma* (1000 CE) and the second, the *Garshāspnāma* (1064–66 CE).

That is not to say that I reject the hypotheses of Y. In fact, they mostly persuade me. And I agree with her overall hypothesis that the *naqqāli* traditions can be traced back to oral traditions in the Ghaznavid era (977–1186 CE). In this regard, her occasional use of sources like the historical narrative of Beyhaqi (d. 1077 CE) helps illuminate the *Sitz im Leben* of such oral traditions. A relevant example is what Beyhaqi has to say about *majālis* 'assemblies' that attend the performances of poets.[20]

16. Nagy 2002:64.
17. Y. p. 40.
18. Y. p. 147–167.
19. Y. p. 27.
20. Fayyāz 1971:360. For a translation see Bosworth and Ashtiany 2011:1.383. Y. p. 54n4 mentions this reference by Beyhaqi, but she ignores the significance of such references at p. 79n76 when she dismisses as "idiosyncratic" the textual variant *anjoman* 'assemblies' at *Shāhnāma* 3.6.9 Bertels. I discuss this passage in Davidson 2013a[1994]:21. On the Persian word

But the question of usefulness remains. Are the hypotheses concerning the "installment divisions" of the *Shāhnāma* and the *Garshāspnāma* really useful in advancing the overall argumentation concerning the "oral background" of these Persian "epics," as the title of the book promises? Yes, perhaps they would be useful, in the larger context of a thorough understanding of the "oral background." In some contexts, as in Y.'s analysis of the narrative about Rostam and Sohrāb in the *tumār* of Zariri, there are signs of such an understanding. When Y. says that "a great deal of planning has gone into the global organisation of the story,"[21] she is showing her awareness that the process of composition in oral traditions is a process of organization. In other contexts, however, there are signs of lapses in her understanding of oral tradition.

At several points in her argumentation, Y. assumes that the process of composition in oral traditions is disorganized and lacking in purpose. This assumption keeps recurring in contexts where she contrasts the composition of the *Shāhnāma* by Ferdowsi. The creative process of such a composition, she thinks, is incompatible with whatever process is involved in the composing of oral poetry.

Y. states at the beginning of her book: "it is not our intention to argue that the [*Shāhnāma* of Ferdowsi] is an oral epic."[22] What she means by "oral," as it soon becomes apparent, is overly narrow because of two basic misunderstandings:

1. Oral poetry, as she understands it, is something that is incompatible with "conscious design and artistic purposes,"[23] such as what we see in the poetry of Ferdowsi. She thinks of oral poetry as a foil for "Ferdowsi's conscious design of his work,"[24] which is characterized by "elaborate artistry and an artistic scheme of interconnections and cross-references."[25] For Y., oral poetry is a "straw man," devoid of any such characteristics as we see them in the poetry of Ferdowsi.

2. Oral poetry, as she understands it, is incompatible with written poetry.

There is no good excuse for the first of these two misunderstandings, since Y. has read enough of Albert Lord to know better. Before I elaborate

---

anjoman as a synonym of *majlis* 'assembly' in contexts of referring to the audiences of poets, see Brookshaw 2003.

21. Y. p. 36.
22. Y. p. xxi.
23. Y. p. xxi.
24. Y. p. xxiii.
25. Y. p. 9.

on what I mean, however, I need to moderate my criticism of the second misunderstanding. In this case, I can find more of an excuse for Y., since Lord's formulations about orality and literacy can more easily be misunderstood. Still, even in this case, there is no good excuse for neglecting to trace the progress made in studies of oral traditions in the course of over forty years since the original publication of Lord's *Singer of Tales* in 1960. It is symbolic of such neglect that Y. in her 2003 book is still using the original 1960 edition of Lord's book and has ignored the 2000 edition, the introduction to which gives an updating about the relevant research concerning orality and literacy.[26] It is now generally understood by experts in oral poetry that orality and literacy are not incompatible in many oral traditions.[27] The later publications of Lord himself make it clear that he, too, had such a general understanding.[28] For Y. to keep on claiming that orality and literacy are incompatible—and to cite the 1960 book of Lord in making such a claim—is to ignore the ongoing progress that has been made in the study of oral traditions around the world.

With that said, I return to the first of the two misunderstandings. Here is what I mean when I say that Y. should have known better. I find it disturbing that a book published in 2003 on oral poetics should still be operating on the assumption that the process of composition in oral poetry is without "conscious design and artistic purposes," to use the phrasing of Y. And I find it even more disturbing to read the inferences made by Y. about Homeric poetry, which had served as the basis for the research of Parry and Lord in their efforts to understand the workings of oral poetry in written texts. Y. claims that the factor of performance has been "overlooked" by those who apply "oral-formulaic theory,"[29] and she goes on to say that "in the absence of contextual information there is no way of telling whether Homer was an oral singer."[30] To back up this claim, Y. refers to the work of Ruth Finnegan and John M. Foley.[31] In the case of Foley, she says that he "accidentally encountered" the disciplines of (1) the "ethnography of speaking" and (2) "ethnopoetics," adding that he has "moved away from the Parry-Lord theory."[32] I doubt that Foley would agree.[33] In any case, what she says about

26. Lord 2000[1960], with a new introduction by Stephen Mitchell and Gregory Nagy at pp. vii–xxix.

27. Nagy 2001.

28. See especially Lord 1991 and 1995. The second of these two books is not cited at all by Y. As for Y.'s selective use of the first book, I will have more to say presently.

29. Y. pp. 18–19.

30. Y. p. 19.

31. Y. pp. 18–19.

32. Y. p. 19n69.

33. I should add that Foley has given me the opportunity of presenting an overview of

the work of Parry and Lord on Homer is mistaken. The fact is, the foundation of their work was and always has been "the factor of performance."[34] It is pointless for Y. to claim that she has found an "alternative approach to the study of oral tradition" by recognizing the fact that "the factor of performance" is "what ultimately distinguishes oral literature from written literature."[35]

For Parry and Lord, composition in oral poetry is a matter of composition-in-performance. It is relevant that Y. criticizes Lord for a distinction he makes in his 1991 book between improvisation and composition-in-performance.[36] Lord here is using the word "improvisation" in a special way in order to make a point. The point is, an unsystematic process of free-association—to which he refers as "improvisation"—is to be distinguished from the systematic process that he calls composition-in-performance. Y. seizes on the fact that Lord in his 1960 book had occasion to use the word "improvise" in a more general sense.[37] That is, he used "improvise" there as a synonym of "compose-in-performance." In my opinion, Y. misses the point that Lord was trying to make "some twenty years after the publication of *The Singer of Tales*" (in terms of the 1991 book, Y. could have said "some thirty years after"). As a former student of Lord, I can attest that he was fond of making distinctions by applying a particular usage of a given word in the context of a particular argument. In such situations, he would give his listeners fair warning that he was proceeding from the general to the particular, just as he gives his readers fair warning in the formulation that is being misread here by Y.

Moving beyond Y.'s disagreements with Lord, we come to the central problem that she has with the application of oral poetics to Persian poetry. In assuming that oral poetry is incompatible with written poetry, Y. also assumes an incompatibility with the concept of the book as articulated in the poetry of Ferdowsi. By contrast, I have argued in both my first book and in the first edition of the present book that there is no such incompatibility.[38] Y. counter-argues by claiming that the *Shāhnāma* of Ferdowsi, as a book, cannot be an "oral" composition. She begins her counter-argument

---

Iranian "epic," in which I summarize the evidence for the oral poetic foundations of this form of poetry (Davidson 2005).

34. For a list of ten concepts of oral poetics that are applicable to Homeric poetry, see Nagy 1996a:16–19; see also his pp. 19–27 for a list of ten examples of common misunderstandings about the oral poetic character of Homeric poetry. An example of outdated views on the characteristics of oral poetry in the Homeric text is what Y. has to say about enjambment (p. 8n31). For an example of more updated views on enjambment, see Clark 1997.

35. Y. p. 139.

36. Y. p. 17; Lord 1991:76.

37. Lord 2000[1960]:118.

38. See especially Essays Two through Four of the present book.

by defining "oral" in the narrowest possible terms and then by associating my arguments with her narrow definition. Already at the beginning of her book, she says: "[Davidson] attempted to interpret the [*Shāhnāma*] as an oral composition."[39] By contrast, she says that her own argument claims only that the *Shāhnāma* and the *Garshāspnāma* were "influenced by oral traditions."[40] In my opinion, this formulation is insufficient. I argue instead that these poetic compositions were actually based on oral traditions, and I understand "oral" in the broadest possible terms. Such a broad understanding is defended in the present book, the first edition of which is cited only erratically by Y., who seems to have started to consult it only after the book version of her thesis was nearly finished. Here is how Y. describes her late discovery of my relevant work: "The present writer is grateful to Dr Julie Scott Meisami for [*sic*] Davidson 2000 and for allowing her to consult her unpublished review of the book."[41]

Y. also has problems with Ferdowsi's references to his "sources," as she describes them, which "sometimes refer to oral traditions, sometimes to written texts, or to both at the same time."[42] She gives nine passages as examples.[43] In the ninth of these (*Shāhnāma* 3.169.2581 Bertels), we see a reference to the *Shāhnāma* as a book. Y. claims that I "disregarded" such passages—except for a passage where Ferdowsi speaks of an archetypal book as the ultimate source of his *Shāhnāma* (1.21.126–136 Bertels).[44] My analysis of that particular passage, I should note, was central for my own argumentation about the oral poetic foundations of the *Shāhnāma*.[45] What, then, makes the ninth passage selected by Y. so special for her? It is the fact that this particular passage does not mention any performance of the poetry contained in the book. But there is nothing special about such passages where the *Shāhnāma* is figured simply as a book. And it is wrong for Y. to say that I disregarded these kinds of passages in the *Shāhnāma*, since I did in fact cite others like it.[46] The real problem for Y. is that there is also a different way for the *Shāhnāma* to refer to itself as a book. I have in mind those passages in the *Shāhnāma* where the idea of a book is a metaphor that expresses the idea of authentically performing the *Shāhnāma* as poetry.[47] And the problem is,

39. Y. p. xxi.

40. Y. p. xxiv.

41. Y. p. xxin14. For more on the views of Meisami, I refer to my notes in Essay Four of the present book.

42. Y. p. 61.

43. Y. pp. 61–67.

44. Y. pp. 66–67.

45. Davidson 2013a[1994]:42–45.

46. Davidson 2013a[1994]:35–36, pointing to *Shāhnāma* 1.23.155–161 Bertels.

47. Davidson 2013a[1994]:17, pointing to *Shāhnāma* 6.136.9–15 Bertels.

Y. denies the existence of such a metaphor. According to her, the last of the nine passages she cites with reference to the "sources" of Ferdowsi shows that "the book as a metaphor for oral authenticity simply does not work."[48] Such a line of reasoning is flawed. Y. is assuming that a metaphor can exist only if the word that is used to express that metaphor is always used that way. It is as if the metaphor of the book as a stylized performance can "work" only if that metaphor is made explicit each and every time a book is mentioned by the poet.

Although she rejects the idea that the *Shāhnāma*, as a book, can be seen as a stylized performance, Y. cannot quite bring herself to accept the alternative idea—that this book is derived from a previous book ascribed to a historical figure by the name of Abu Manṣur.[49] After reviewing what scholars like Nöldeke, Qazvini, and Minorsky have to say in favor of that idea, she sides with the reservations of Blois[50] in concluding: "The assumption that Abu Manṣur's [*Shāhnāma*] was Ferdowsi's source is based on somewhat precarious grounds."[51] Such assumptions turn out to be too "speculative" for her[52]. She also distances herself from another alternative idea—as advocated by Blois—involving multiple textual sources.[53]

Given all her reservations about such arguments for textual sources, we would expect Y. to consider the possibility that the *Shāhnāma* was derived from oral poetry. But her narrow understanding of oral poetry prevents her from going that far, and she adopts a neutral position. Unfortunately for me, my work becomes the foil for this position: "Davidson's argument is unconvincing."[54] And what is the problem with the argument? Primarily, it is this: "She assumed that the [*Shāhnāma*] was oral poetry as defined by the Oral-Formulaic Theory."[55] And, secondarily, Y. has two other related problems: (1) as we have already seen, I supposedly "disregarded" passages that refer to the *Shāhnāma* simply as a book,[56] and (2) I "over-interpreted" the meaning of some words, such as *sarāyanda*.[57]

48. Y. p. 67.
49. Y. p. 63.
50. Y. p. xx, 6n23.
51. Y. p. 3.
52. Y. p. 7.
53. Y. p. 7n27. On the arguments presented by Nöldeke, Qazvini, Minorsky, and Blois concerning the book of Abu Manṣur and other possible sources for the *Shāhnāma*, I refer to Davidson 2001.
54. Y. p. 65.
55. Y. p. 63. For a critique of the term "oral-formulaic theory," see Nagy 1996a:19–20.
56. Y. pp. 66–67.
57. Y. p. 66. At a later point in her argumentation, however, Y. (p. 78n75) distances herself

As a justification for her neutral position, Y. provides a lengthy table indicating the distribution of Ferdowsi's references to his "sources."[58] And what can we infer from this table? It is difficult to tell. I cannot make sense of her summary of the results. At one point, she says: "What ultimately matters, therefore, is the regularity and consistency with which Ferdowsi associated given stories with ancient (and possibly oral) traditions."[59] But where is the regularity and consistency? There seems to be none, if we follow her own formulation: "Ferdowsi gave little thought to clearly distinguishing oral sources from the written, leaving us with equivocal remarks that can refer to both sources."[60] For Y., the concept of "oral sources" applies especially to the poetic tradition represented by stories stemming from Sistān.[61] And it is these stories from Sistān that lead Y. to put into words the dilemma that her argumentation has created for her:

> Although these stories have been attributed [by Nöldeke] to unidentified written texts in possession of Ferdowsi, they could just as well be oral. Here the oral and written distinction reaches the level of absurdity; and yet Ferdowsi leaves us with the impression that the stories have been transmitted orally.[62]

I sympathize with Y.'s reaction. Yes, the distinction does seem absurd. I would even say that it is in fact absurd—but only because Y.'s view of what is "oral" is overly narrow.

Y.'s dilemma could perhaps be solved if she adopted a broader view. Part of the solution, I suggest, would be for her to reconsider the relevant narratives concerning the genesis of an archetypal book that disintegrates and is then later reintegrated under the leadership of a wise defender of traditions. I have already referred to my analysis of the most elaborate version of such a narrative: it is the passage where Ferdowsi describes the genesis of an archetypal book that becomes the ultimate source of his *Shāhnāma* (1.21.126–136 Bertels). As I have argued, "Ferdowsi's description of this genesis amounts to a myth-made stylization of oral poetry."[63] We find many variations on this theme of the disintegrated and then reintegrated book, including a story to

---

from her negative comments on my analysis of *sarāyanda*, citing my detailed analysis of this word in first edition of the present book.

58. Y. pp. 68–73.
59. Y. p. 76.
60. Y. p. 100.
61. In this regard, her remarks at p. 75n64 are most helpful.
62. Y. p. 74.
63. Davidson 2005:268.

which I referred earlier concerning Abu Manṣur and his prose *Shāhnāma*.[64] Also comparable is the story about the *Zartoshtnāma* or 'Book of Zoroaster', as noted by Y. herself.[65]

Furthermore, Y.'s work also indicates that the medieval Persian narratives about a disintegrated and then reintegrated book can be traced back to earlier Iranian narratives. Already in the ancient Avestan tradition, a book could be seen as the foundation of performance. A case in point is a passage of the *Dēnkard*, 'Acts of Religion', which is a 10th-century Middle Persian compendium of Zoroastrian beliefs and customs.[66] The passage of the *Dēnkard* in question relates the transmission of archetypal Avestan texts—texts that date back ultimately to the second millennium BCE. According to this story, three pivotal moments in the transmission happened in three successive eras of Iranian imperial kingship. The three eras are represented by three kings who stem from three successive Iranian dynasties, which are the Achaemenid (item 1), the Parthian (item 2), and the Sasanian (item 3):

(1) Daray, son of Daray, [= Darius III] commanded that two written copies of all Avesta and Zand, even as Zardusht [= Zoroaster] had received them from Ohrmazd [= Ahura Mazda], be preserved ...

(2) Valakhsh the Ashkanian [= Vologases I] commanded that a memorandum be sent to the provinces (instructing them) to preserve, in the state in which they had come down in (each) province, whatever had survived in purity of the Avesta and Zand as well as every teaching derived from it which, scattered through the land of Iran by the havoc and disruption of Alexander, and by the pillage and plundering of the Macedonians, had remained authoritative, whether written or in oral transmission.

(3) His Majesty Ardashir, King of kings, son of Pāpak [= Ardashir I], acting on the just judgement of Tansār, demanded that all those scattered teachings should be brought to the court. Tansār assumed command, and selected those that were trustworthy, and left the rest out of the canon.[67]

In brief, the ancient Avestan tradition is seen in terms of a book that

64. More in Davidson 2005:268–272.

65. Y. p. 5n17, with bibliography referring to my analysis of that story.

66. The passage in question is discussed by Y. at p. 5.

67. Boyce 1984:114. As I emphasize by separating the text into three distinct segments, there is a spanning of three consecutive dynasties in this narrative. The Achaemenid dynasty is represented by Darius III (ruled 336–330 BCE), the Parthian by the king Vologases I (ruled 51–78 CE), and the Sasanian by Ardashir I (ruled 208–242 CE).

serves as the foundation of performance. So the medieval Persian narrative of Ferdowsi's *Shāhnāma* about a disintegrated and then reintegrated book can be traced back to earlier Iranian traditions: the Avestan texts were likewise 'scattered through the land of Iran'. There is therefore a deep prehistory to be found in the linkage of book and performance.[68]

There is also a wealth of additional evidence for such linkage to be found in the material culture of the medieval Persian manuscript traditions themselves. I have in mind here the dynamic new research emanating from the Cambridge-Edinburgh Shahnama Project. Robert Hillenbrand has recently edited a volume of important papers stemming from this research.[69] His own chapter in the volume, "New Perspectives in Shahnama Iconography," is most relevant to the issues raised here in my essay.[70] Equally relevant is the important chapter by Marianne Shreve Simpson, "Shahnama as Text and Shahnama as Image."[71] As we learn from these and other chapters in the volume, there was a collaborative relationship between scribe and painter in producing illustrated versions of the *Shāhnāma*: the scribe copied out the text by hearing it dictated to him, while the painter painted illustrations that were thematically relevant to what was being dictated. And the thematic variations we see in the paintings can be matched with thematic variations in the textual transmission by way of dictation. The point is, such variations in the textual transmission can be explained in terms of variations in oral transmission. For some time now, as Simpson points out, art historians who specialize in the fourteenth-century manuscripts of the *Shāhnāma*, with all their textual variations, have appreciated such an explanation: "Interestingly, efforts by literary historians to place the Shahnama in the context of oral poetics and production do happen to coincide with tentative suggestions made by art historians some time ago when confronted with the range of textual variants in fourteenth-century illustrated volumes of [Ferdowsi's] epic."[72] When it comes to "investigations of the oral aspect of the Shahnama" as undertaken by myself and others, Simpson notes that they "have not been without their detractors," since "they seem to undermine [Ferdowsi's] role as the author of an original, written text."[73]

I conclude by expressing the hope that Y. will consider making a second

68. I discuss this Pahlavi passage in the context of a multiplicity of comparable narratives in my forthcoming essay entitled "Parallel Heroic Themes in the Medieval Irish *Cattle Raid of Cooley* and the Medieval Persian *Book of Kings*."

69. Hillenbrand 2004b.

70. Hillenbrand 2004a.

71. Simpson 2004.

72. Simpson 2004:10.

73. Simpson 2004:10.

edition of her book. Her work is too valuable to be marred by an overly narrow view of oral poetics. I hope that this essay has helped point the way toward achieving a broader view. The criticisms I have made are meant to be constructive, and they are offered in the larger context of my admiration for all the industry and ingenuity that went into this important book.

Bibliography

Abdesselem, M. 1977. *Le thème de la mort*. Tunis.

Abu-Lughod, L. 1985. "Honor and Sentiments of Loss in a Bedouin Society." *American Ethnologist* 12:245–261.

——. 1999. *Veiled Sentiments: Honor and Poetry in a Bedouin Society*. Berkeley. 2nd ed. Orig. pub. 1986.

Alexiou, M. 2002. *The Ritual Lament in Greek Tradition*. Cambridge, MA. 2nd ed. Ed. Dimitrios Yatromanolakis and Panagiotis Roilos. Orig. pub. 1974.

Alishan, L. P. 1989. "Rostamica I: On the Epithet *tāj.bakhsh*." *Studia Iranica* 18:3–26.

Allen, T. W. 1902–1912. *Homeri Opera*. 5 vols. Oxford.

Austin, J. L. 1975. *How to do Things with Words*. 2nd ed. Ed. J. O. Urmson and Marina Sbisà. Oxford.

Bate, W. J. 1970. *The Burden of the Past and the English Poet*. Cambridge, MA.

Bertels, Y. E. et al. 1960–1971. *Ferdowsi. Shakhname*. 9 vols. Moscow.

Bivar, A. D. H. 1980–1981. "Gondophares and the *Shāhnāma*." *Iranica Antiqua* 15–16:141–151.

Blackburn, S. H. 1989. "Patterns of Development for Indian Oral Epics." In *Oral Epics in India*, ed. S. H. Blackburn, P. J. Claus, J. B. Flueckiger, and S. S. Wadley, 15-32. Berkeley.

Blois, F. de. 1990. *Burzōy's Voyage to India and the Origin of the Book of* Kalīlah wa Dimnah. London.

——. 1998. Review of Davidson 1994. *Journal of the Royal Asiatic Society* 8:269–270.

——. 2004. *Persian Literature: A Bio-Bibliographical Survey. Volume 5. Poetry of the Pre-Mongol Period*. 3 fascs. 2nd ed. London. Orig. pub. 1992–1997.

Bosworth, C.E. 2011. *The History of Beyhaqi*. Ed. Mohsen Ashtiany. Boston.

Boyce, M. 1954. *The Manichaean Hymn-Cycles in Parthian*. London.

——. 1955. "Zariadres and Zarer." *Bulletin of the School of Oriental and African Studies* 17:463–477.

——. 1957. "The Parthian *Gōsān* and the Iranian Minstrel Tradition." *Journal of the Royal Asiatic Society* 18:10–45.

——. 1975. "On Varuna's Part in Zoroastrianism." In Moïnfar 1975:57–66.

——. 1975–82. *A History of Zoroastrianism*. Vols. 1, *The Early Period*, and 2. *Under the Achaemenians*. Handbuch der Orientalistik 1.8.2.2a. Leiden.

——. 1984. *Textual Sources for the Study of Zoroastrianism*. Manchester.

——. 1986. "Apąm Napāt." *Encyclopaedia Iranica* 2:148–150.
Brookshaw, D. P. 2003. "Palaces, Pavilions and Pleasure-Gardens: The Context and Setting of the Medieval *majlis*." *Middle Eastern Literatures* 6:199–223.
Brough, J. 1959. "The tripartite ideology of the Indo-Europeans: An experiment in method." *Bulletin of the School of Oriental and African Studies* 22:68–86.
Caraveli, A. 1986. "The Bitter Wounding: Lament as a Social Protest in Rural Greece." In *Gender and Power in Rural Greece*, ed. J. Dubisch, 169–194. Princeton.
Clark, M. 1997. *Out of Line: Homeric Composition beyond the Hexameter*. Lanham.
Coutau-Bégaire, H. 1998. *L'oeuvre de Georges Dumézil: Catalogue raisonné*. Paris.
Danforth, L. 1982. *The Death Rituals of Rural Greece*. Princeton.
Darmesteter, J. 1887. "Points de contact entre le *Mahābhārata* et le *Shāhnāmeh*." *Journal Asiatique* 2:38–75.
Davidson, O. M. 1980. "Indo-European Dimensions of Herakles in *Iliad* 19.95–133." *Arethusa* 13.2, *Indo-European Roots of Classical Culture*, 197–202.
——. 1985. "The Crown-Bestower and the Iranian Book of Kings." *Acta Iranica* 10, *Papers in Honour of Professor Mary Boyce*, 61–148.
——. 1988. "Formulaic Analysis of Samples taken from the *Shāhnāma* of Ferdowsi." *Oral Tradition* 3:88–105.
——. 1990. "The *Haft Khwān* Tradition as an Intertextual Phenomenon in Ferdowsi's *Shāhnāma*." *Bulletin of the Asia Institute* 4, *In of Honor of Richard N. Frye: Aspects Iranian Culture*, ed. C. A. Bromberg, Bernard Goldman, P. O. Skjærvø, and A. S. Shahbazi, 209-215.
——. 1998a. "Epic as a Frame for Speech-Acts: Ritual Boasting in the *Shāhnāma* of Ferdowsi." In *Neue Methoden der Epenforschung*, ScriptOralia 59, ed. H. L. C. Tristram, 271–285. Tübingen.
——. 1998b. "The Text of Ferdowsi's *Shāhnāma* and the Burden of the Past." *Journal of the American Oriental Society* 118:63–68.
——. 1998c. "Women's Lament as Protest in the Persian Book of Kings." In *Women in the Medieval Islamic World*, ed. Gavin R. G. Hambly, The New Middle Ages 6, ed. B. Wheeler, 131–146. New York.
——. 2001."Some Iranian Poetic Tropes as Reflected in the 'Life of Ferdowsi' Traditions." In *Philologica et Linguistica: Festschrift für Helmut Humbach*, ed. M. G. Schmidt and W. Bisang, Supplement 1–12. Trier.
——. 2002. "Haft K̲vān." *Encyclopaedia Iranica* 11:516–519.
——. 2005. "Persian/Iranian Epic." In *A Companion to Ancient Epic*, ed. J. M. Foley, 264–276. Malden.

——. 2008. Review of Yamamoto 2003. *Orientalistische Literaturzeitung* 103.3:305–316.

——. 2013a. *Poet and Hero in the Persian Book of Kings*. 3rd ed. Boston and Washington. Orig. pub. 1994.

——. 2013b. *Comparative Literature and Classical Persian Poetics*. 2nd ed. Boston and Washington. Orig. pub. 2000.

——. Forthcoming. "Parallel Heroic Themes in the Medieval Irish *Cattle Raid of Cooley* and the Medieval Persian *Book of Kings*."

Davis, D. 1992. *Epic and Sedition: The Case of Ferdowsi's Shāhnāmeh*. Fayetteville.

——. 1995a. Review of Davidson 1994. *Times Literary Supplement* February 3, *Middle East: "Orientalism Revisited,"* 11.

——. 1995b. Review of Khaleghi-Motlagh 1992. *International Journal of Middle East Studies* 27:393–395.

——. 1996. "The Problem of Ferdowsi's Sources." *Journal of the American Oriental Society* 116:48–57.

Duchesne-Guillemin, J. 1963. "Le *Xvarenah*." *Annali dell' Istituto Orientale di Napoli, Sezione Linguistica* 5:19–31.

Dumézil, G. 1959. "L'idéologie tripartie des Indo-Européens et la Bible." *Kratylos* 4:97–118.

——. 1968–1973. *Mythe et épopée*. 3 vols. Paris. Repr. 1995 with foreword by J. Grisward.

Dustx^{v}āh, J. 1990. *Morshed ʿAbbās Zariri. Dāstān-e Rostam va Sohrāb: Revāyat-e Naqqālān*. Tehran.

Elwell-Sutton, L. P. 1976. *The Persian Metres*. Cambridge.

Eribon, D. 1992. *Faut-il brûler Dumézil? Mythologie, science et politique*. Paris.

Fahd T. 1995. "Niyāḥa." *Encyclopedia of Islam* 8, 2nd ed., 64–65.

Fayyāz, A. 1971. *Tarikh-e Beyhaqi*. Mashhad.

Feld, S. 1990. *Birds, Weeping, Poetics and Song in Kululi Expression*. 2nd ed. Philadelphia.

Ford, P. K. 1974. "The Well of Nechtan and 'La Gloire Lumineuse'." In *Myth in Indo-European Antiquity*, ed. G. I. Larson, 67-74. Berkeley.

Frye, R. N. 1995. Review of Davidson 1994. *Harvard Middle Eastern and Islamic Review* 2.2:128–129.

Gershenson, D. 1991. *Apollo the Wolf-God*. McLean, VA.

Grima, B. 1992. *The Performance of Emotion among the Paxtun Women: "The Misfortunes which Have Befallen Me."* Austin, TX.

Guillén, C. 1985. *Entre lo uno y lo diverso. Introducción a la literatura comparada*. Barcelona.

——. 1993. *The Challenge of Comparative Literature.* Havard Studies in Comparative Literature 42. Cambridge, MA.
Heesterman, J. C. 1957. *The Ancient Indian Royal Consecration.* The Hague.
Henning, W. B. 1942. "The Disintegration of Avestic Studies." *Transactions of the Philological Society* 1942:40–56.
——. 1950. "A Pahlavi Poem." *Bulletin of the School of Oriental and African Studies* 13:641–648.
Herrmann, G. 1997. Review of Davidson 1994. *Central Asiatic Journal* 41:127–128.
Herzfeld, M. 1993. "In Defiance of Destiny: the Management of Time and Gender at a Cretan Funeral." *American Ethnologist* 20:241–255.
Hillenbrand, R., ed. 2004a. "New Perspectives in *Shahnama* Iconography." In Hillenbrand 2004b:1–7.
——. 2004b. Shahnama*: the Visual Language of the Persian Book of Kings.* VARIE Occasional Papers 2. Aldershot.
Holst-Warhaft, G. 1992. *Dangerous Voices: Women's Lament and Greek Literature.* London.
Humbach, H., and Skjærvø, P. O. 1978–83. *The Sassanian Inscription of Paikuli.* 3 vols. Wiesbaden.
Huot, S. 1991. "Chronicle, Lai, and Romance: Orality and Writing in the *Roman de Perceforest.*" In *Vox Intexta: Orality and Textuality in the Middle Ages*, ed. A. N. Doane and C. B. Pasternack, 203–223. Madison, WI.
Jamison, S. W. 1991. *The Ravenous Hyenas and the Wounded Sun: Myth and Ritual in Ancient India.* Ithaca.
Kassis, K. 1979. *Moirológia tês Mánês.* Vol. 1. Athens.
Khaleghi-Motlagh, Dj. 1988–2008. *Abū'l-Qāsem Ferdowsī. Shāhnāmeh.* 8 vols. New York.
Kianush, M. 1996. Review of Davidson 1994. *Asian Affairs* October 2:1.
Kieffer, C. M. 1975. "Les formules de lamentation funèbre des femmes à Caboul: *awåz andåxtan-e zan* ." In Moïnfar 1975:313–323.
Kubler-Ross, E. 1969. *On Death and Dying.* New York.
Lathuillère, R. 1966. *Giron le courtois: Étude de la tradition manuscrite et analyse critique.* Geneva.
Lazard, G. 1975. "The Rise of the New Persian Language." *Cambridge History of Iran* 4:595-657. Cambridge.
Lord, A. B. 1986. "Perspectives on Recent Work on the Oral Traditional Formula." *Oral Tradition* 1:467–503.
——. 1991. *Epic Singers and Oral Tradition.* Ithaca.
——. 1995. *The Singer Resumes the Tale.* Ithaca.
——. 2000. *The Singer of Tales.* 2nd ed. Ed. S. Mitchell and G. Nagy. Cambridge, MA. Orig. pub. 1960.

Louden, Bruce. 1999. "Bacchylides 17: Theseus and Indo-Iranian Apâm Napât." *Journal of Indo-European Studies* 27:57–78.

Lutz, C. 1986. "Emotion, Thought, and Estrangement: Emotion as a Cultural Category." *Cultural Anthropology* 1:287–309.

Maguire, M. 1973. *Rustam and Isfandiyar in the* Shahnameh. PhD diss., Princeton University.

Martin, R. P. 1989. *The Language of Heroes: Speech and Performance in the Iliad.* Ithaca.

Marzolph, U. 2002. "The Persian National Epic in between Tradition and Ideology." In *The Kalevala and the World's Traditional Epics*, Studia Fennica Folkloristica 12, ed. Lauri Honko, 276–293. Helsinki.

Meisami, J. S. 1987. *Medieval Persian Court Poetry.* Princeton.

——. 1993. "The Past in Service of the Present: Two Views of History in Medieval Persia." *Poetics Today* 14:247–275.

Minorsky, V. 1964. "The Older Preface of the *Shāh-nama.*" *Iranica, Twenty Articles*, Publications of the University of Tehran 755, 260–274. Tehran.

Mohl, J. 1838–1878. *Le livre des rois.* 7 vols. Paris.

Moïnfar, D., ed. 1975. *Mélanges linguistiques offerts à Emile Benveniste.* Leuven.

Mokri, M. 1995. "Pleureuses professionelles et la mort de Chīrīn: Lamentations funéraires en Iran occidental (chez les Kurdes)." *Contributions scientifiques aux études iraniennes* 4, *Persico-Kurdica*, 460-505.

Monroe, J. 1972. "Oral Composition in Pre-Islamic Poetry." *Journal of Arabic Literature* 3:1–53.

Muellner, M. 1976. *The Meaning of Homeric EYXOMAI through its Formulas.* Innsbruck.

——. 1990. "The Simile of the Cranes and Pygmies: A Study of Homeric Metaphor." *Harvard Studies in Classical Philology* 93:59–101.

Nagy, G. 1980. "Patroklos, Concepts of Afterlife, and the Indic Triple Fire." *Arethusa* 13:161–195.

——. 1990a. *Greek Mythology and Poetics.* Ithaca.

——. 1990b. *Pindar's Homer: The Lyric Possession of an Epic Past.* Baltimore.

——. 1996a. *Homeric Questions.* Austin, TX.

——. 1996b. *Poetry as Performance: Homer and Beyond.* Cambridge.

——. 1997. "An Inventory of Debatable Assumptions about a Homeric Question." *Bryn Mawr Classical Review* 97.4.18.

——. 1998. "Aristarchean Questions." *Bryn Mawr Classical Review* 98.7.14.

——. 1999a. *The Best of the Achaeans: Concepts of the Hero in Archaic Greek Poetry.* Baltimore. 2nd ed. Orig. pub. 1979.

——. 1999b. "Homer and Plato at the Panathenaia: Synchronic and Diachronic Perspectives." In *Contextualizing Classics*, ed. T. M. Falkner, N. Felson, and D. Konstan, 127-155. Lanham.

——. 2001. "Orality and Literacy." *Encyclopedia of Rhetoric*, ed. T. O. Sloane, 532–538. Oxford.

——. 2002. *Plato's Rhapsody and Homer's Music: The Poetics of the Panathenaic Festival in Classical Athens*. Washington, DC.

Nagy, J. F. 1985. *The Wisdom of the Outlaw: The Boyhood Deeds of Finn in Gaelic Narrative Tradition*. Berkeley.

Nöldeke, Th. 1930. *The Iranian National Epic*. Trans. L. Bogdanov. Mumbai.

Oettinger, N. 2009. "Zum Verhältnis von Apąm Napāt und Xvarənah im Avesta." In *Zarathushtra entre l'Inde et l'Iran: Etudes indo-iraniennes et indo-européennes offertes à Jean Kellens à l'occasion de son 65e anniversaire*, ed. É. Pirart and X. Tremblay, 189–196. Wiesbaden.

Okpewho, I. 1979. *The Epic in Africa: Toward a Poetics of the Oral Performance*. New York.

Oldenberg, H. 1917. *Die Religion des Veda*. 2nd ed. Stuttgart.

Omidsalar, M. 1996. "Unburdening Ferdowsi." *Journal of the American Oriental Society* 116:235–242.

——. 2002. "Orality, mouvance, and editorial theory in Shāhnāma Studies." *Jerusalem Studies in Arabic and Islam* 27:245–282.

——. 2011. *Poetics and Politics of Iran's National Epic, the* Shāhnāmeh. New York.

Page, M. E. 1977. *Naqqāli and Ferdowsi: Creativity in the Iranian National Tradition*. PhD diss., University of Pennsylvania.

——. 1979. "Professional Storytelling in Iran: Transmission and Practice." *Iranian Studies* 12:195–215.

Parks, W. 1986. "Flyting and Fighting: Pathways in the Realization of the Epic Contest." *Neophilologus* 70:292–306.

——. 1990. *Verbal Dueling in Heroic Narrative: The Homeric and Old English Traditions*. Princeton.

Parry, A., ed. 1971. *The Making of Homeric Verse: The Collected Papers of Milman Parry*. Oxford.

Parry, M. 1928a. *L'épithète traditionnelle dans Homère: Essai sur un problème de style homérique*. Paris. Trans. in A. Parry 1971:1–190.

——. 1928b. *Les formules et la métrique d'Homère*. Paris. Translated in A. Parry 1971:191–239.

——. 1930. "Studies in the Epic Technique of Oral Verse-Making. 1. Homer and Homeric Style." *Harvard Studies in Classical Philology* 41:73–147. Reprinted in A. Parry 1971:266–324.

——. 1932. "Studies in the Epic Technique of Oral Verse-Making. 2. The Homeric Language as the Language of an Oral Poetry." *Harvard Studies in Classical Philology* 43:1–50. Reprinted in A. Parry 1971:325–364.

Pasquali, G. 1952. *Storia della tradizione e critica del testo*. 2nd ed. Florence.
Pickens, R. T., ed. 1978. *The Songs of Jaufré Rudel*. Toronto.
——. 1994. "'Old' Philology and the Crisis of the 'New'." In *The Future of the Middle Ages: Medieval Literature in the 1990s*, ed. W. D. Paden, 53–86. Gainesville.
Piemontese, A. 1980. "Nuova luce su Firdawsi: Uno *Šāhnāma* datato 614H./1217 a Firenze." *Istituto Orientale a Napoli, Annali* 40:1–38, 189–242.
Puhvel, J. 1973. "*Aquam exstinguere*." *Journal of Indo-European Studies* 1:379–386.
——. 1987. *Comparative Mythology*. Baltimore.
Reichl, K. 1992. *Turkic Oral Epic Poetry: Traditions, Forms, Poetic Structure*. New York.
——. 2000. *Singing the Past: Turkic and Medieval Heroic Poetry*. Ithaca.
Reynolds, D. F. 1995. *Heroic Poets, Poetic Heroes: The Ethnography of Performance in an Arabic Oral Epic Tradition*. Ithaca.
Richards, I. A. 1936. *The Philosophy of Rhetoric*. Oxford.
Rosenblatt, P. C., Walsh, R., and Jackson, A. 1976. *Grief and Mourning in Cross-Cultural Perspective*. New Haven.
Rubanovich, J. 2012. "Orality in Medieval Persian Literature." In *Medieval Oral Literature*, ed. Karl Reichl, 653–679. Berlin.
Russell, J. R. 1987. *Zoroastrianism in Armenia*. Harvard Iranian Series 5. Cambridge, MA.
Ṣafā, Dh. 1984. *Ḥamāsa sarāʾī dar Irān*. Tehran. Orig. pub. 1944.
Sale, W. M. 1993. "Homer and the *Roland*: The Shared Formular Technique." *Oral Tradition* 8:87–142, 381–412.
Sarkārāti, B. 1976–7. "Rostam: Yek Shakhsiyyat-e Tārikhi yā Ostureʾi?" *Majalleh-ye Dāneshkadeh-ye Adabiyyāt wa Ulum-e Ensāni* 12:164–192.
Schmitt, R. 1967. *Dichtung und Dichtersprache in indogermanischer Zeit*. Wiesbaden.
Searle, J. R. 1979. *Expression and Meaning: Studies in Speech-Acts*. Cambridge.
Seremetakis, C. N. 1990. "The Ethics of Antiphony: The Social Construction of Pain, Gender and Power in the Southern Peloponnese." *Ethos* 18:281–511.
Shahbazi, A. S. 1991. *Ferdowsī: A Critical Biography*. Costa Mesa.
Shayegan, R. M. 2011. *Arsacids and Sasanians: Political Ideology in Post-Hellenistic and Late Anqitque Persia*. Cambridge.
——. 2012. *Aspects of History and Epic in Ancient Iran: From Gaumāta to Wahnām*. Cambridge, MA.
Simidchieva, M. 1994. Review of Davidson 1994. *Al-Masāq: Studia Arabo-Islamica Mediterranea* 7:327–331.

Simpson, M. S. 2004. "*Shahnama* as Text and *Shahnama* as Image: A Brief Overview of Recent Studies, 1975–2000." In Hillenbrand 2004b:9–23.

Skjærvø, P. O. 1994. "Hymnic Composition in the *Avesta*." *Die Sprache* 36:199–243.

———. 1996a. "The Literature of the Most Ancient Iranians." *The Journal of the Research and Historical Preservation Committee* 2, *Proceedings of the Second North American Gatha Conference*, ed. S. J. H. Manekshaw and P. R. Ichaporia, 221–235.

———. 1996b. "Zarathustra in the *Avesta* and in Manicheism: Irano-Manichaeica IV." *Accademia Nazionale dei Lincei: Atti dei Convengni Lincei* 127, *La Persia e l'Asia Centrale da Alessandro al X Secolo*, 597–628.

———. 1997a. "Avestica II: Yokes and Spades and Remnants of the 'Tripartite Ideology'." *Münchener Studien zur Sprachwissenschaft* 57:115–128.

———. 1997b. "The State of Old Avestan Scholarship." *Journal of the American Oriental Society* 117:103–114.

———. 1998a. "Eastern Iranian Epic Traditions I: Siyāvaš and Kunāla." In *Mír Curad: Studies in Honor of Calvert Watkins*, ed. J. Jasanoff, H. C. Melchert, and L. Oliver, 645–658.

———. 1998b. "Eastern Iranian Epic Traditions II: Rostam and Bhīṣma." *Acta Orientalia Academiae Scientiarum Hungaricae* 51:159–170.

———. 1998c. "Royalty in Early Iranian Literature." In *Proceedings of the Third European Conference of Iranian Studies*, vol. 1, *Old and Middle Iranian Studies*, ed. N. Sims-Williams, 99–107. Wiesbaden.

Slymovics, S. 1987. *The Merchant of Art: An Egyptian Hilali Oral Epic Poet in Performance*. Berkeley.

Storey, C. A. 1927–. *Persian Literature: A Bio-Bibliographical Survey*.

Vahman, Fereydun and Garnik Asatrian. 1995. *Poetry of the Baxtiārīs: Love Poems, Wedding Songs, Lullabies, Laments*. Copenhagen.

Vidal-Naquet, P. 1992. Review of Eribon 1992. *Le Nouvel Observateur* 1456:114–116.

Watkins, C. 1995. *How to Kill a Dragon: Aspects of Indo-European Poetics*. Oxford.

West, M. L. 2007. *Indo-European Poetry and Myth*. Oxford.

Wickens, G. M. 1995. Review of Davidson 1994. *International Journal of Middle East Studies* 27:528–530.

Wikander, S. 1959. "Sur le fonds commun indo-iranien des épopées de la Perse et de l'Inde." *La Nouvelle Clio* 1:310–329.

Witzel, M. 1987. "The Coronation Rituals of Nepal: With Special Reference to the Coronation of King Birendea (1975)." *Nepalica* 4, *Heritage of the Kathmandu Valley*, ed. N. Gutschow and A. Michaels, 415–468. Sankt Augustin.

Wolff, F. 1935. *Glossar zu Firdousis Schahname*. Berlin.
Yamamoto, K. 2003. *The Oral Background of Persian Epics: Storytelling and Poetry*. Brill Studies in Middle Eastern Literatures 26. Leiden.
Zumthor, P. 1972. *Essai de poétique médiévale*. Paris.
Zwettler, M. 1978. *The Oral Tradition of Classical Arabic Poetry: Its Character and Implications*. Columbus.

Index